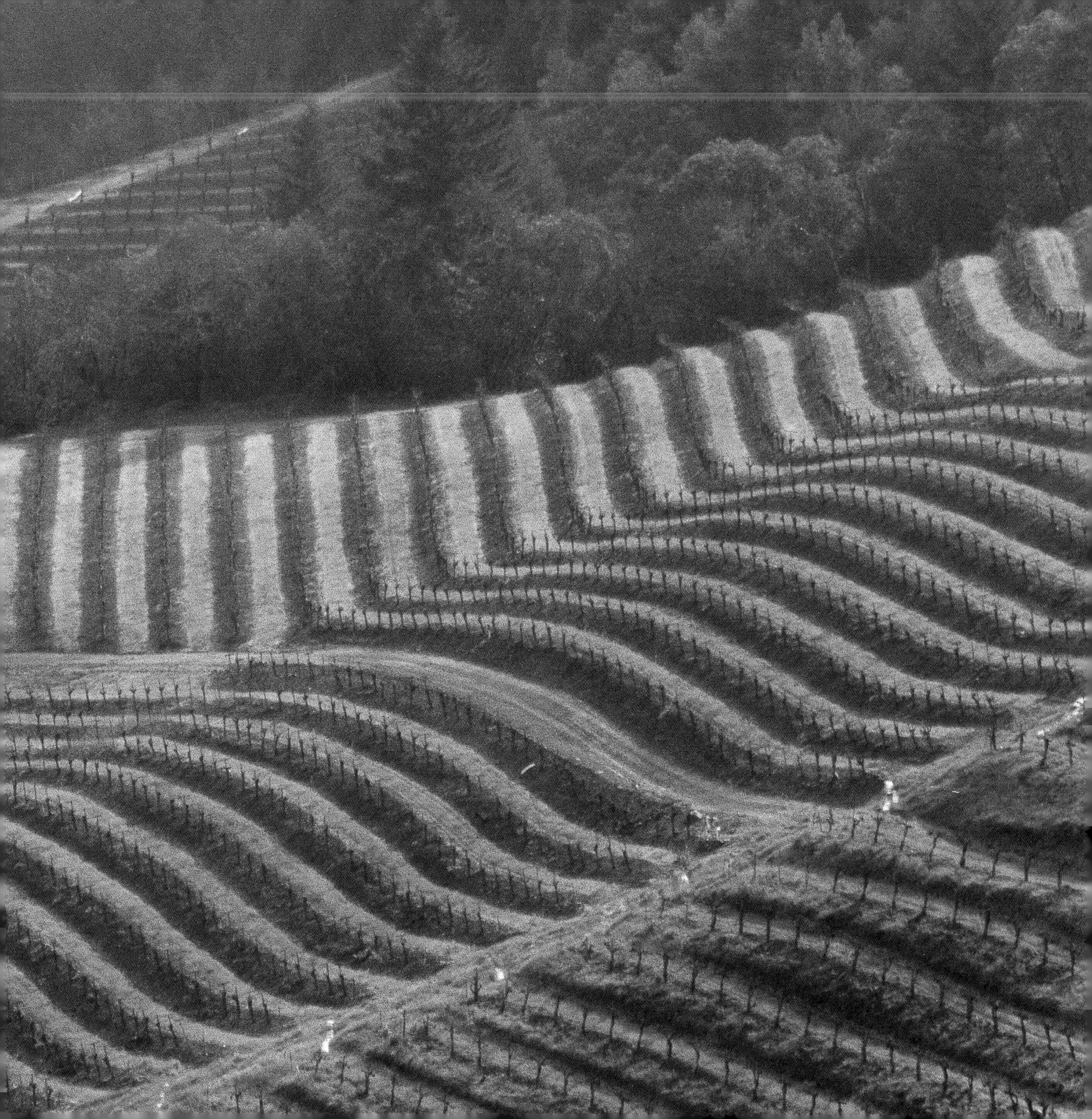

by james mcnair

the sutter home
NAPA VALLEY COOKBOOK

food photography by Zeva Oelbaum
food styling by Jennifer Udell
location photography by M. J. Wickham

CHRONICLE BOOKS
SAN FRANCISCO

Library of Congress Cataloging-in-Publication Data:
   McNair, James K.
      The Sutter Home Napa Valley Cookbook/
      by James McNair; photographs by Zeva Oelbaum.
      p.   cm.
   ISBN 0-8118-2200-1 (pbk.)
   1. Cookery, American—California style.
   2. Sutter Home Winery.   I. Title.

TX715.2.C34 M35 2000
641.59794—dc21
99-053486

       CIP

Printed in Hong Kong.

Prop styling by Barb Fritz
Food styling by Jennifer Udell
Food photography assistance by Effie Paroutsas
Designed by Stefanie Hermsdorf
Typesetting by Stefanie Hermsdorf

Distributed in Canada by Raincoast Books
8680 Cambie Street
Vancouver, British Columbia V6P 6M9

10 9 8 7 6 5 4 3 2 1

Chronicle Books
85 Second Street
San Francisco, California 94105

www.chroniclebooks.com

contents

foreword

On December 5, 1948, my mother, sister, brother, and I arrived in Oakland, California, after a three-day train ride from New York City. Our father, who had come west several months earlier, met us at the station, and we drove north to begin our new lives as vintners in the town of St. Helena in Napa Valley.

My father and uncle had purchased Sutter Home Winery the year before, and as we pulled into the drive, my mother began to cry. The winery, which dated to 1874, but had been abandoned in 1918 as the movement toward Prohibition accelerated, was a dilapidated old barn fronted by a sea of waist-high weeds. It had dirt floors, no electricity, and a collection of sorry-looking tanks and barrels.

Eventually, Mom stopped crying, and we set about reviving the winery. For the next twenty-five years, we operated the quintessential mom-and-pop operation. If you could carry or roll a container through our door, we'd fill it up for you.

Locals joked that Sutter Home made fifty-two different wines, but had only two tanks, one for red wine and one for white. It wasn't far from the truth.

In 1972, sort of by accident, I created a wine called White Zinfandel. It took a decade for it to catch on, but when it did, Sutter Home was transformed from a small family vintner into what it is today: America's largest premium wine producer and its fourth largest winery.

As central to my life as wine has been, the preparation and enjoyment of food has been equally important. Both of my parents grew up in Piedmont, in northwestern Italy, where good food and wine are a way of life. My dad's parents owned a vineyard and later ran a restaurant in the coastal Ligurian town of Savona.

The family immigrated to the United States in the 1920s, settling in New York and New Jersey, where they all worked as cooks, waiters, or bartenders. During Prohibition, the Trincheros operated a hotel and restaurant called the Paradise Inn in upstate New York, where my grandfather made wine in the basement.

After Prohibition, my father returned to Manhattan, met and married my mother, and began working in midtown hotels as a cook and bartender. As a child, I remember big family dinners every weekend, the table crammed with relatives eating, talking, laughing, and drinking wine. My dad, a great cook, would prepare his specialties: gnocchi, polenta with rabbit sausage, veal scallopini, chicken cacciatore, and leg of lamb seasoned with garlic and rosemary. There was always a gallon jug of wine on the table.

Over the years, I inherited my father's pleasure in cooking. Like my mother, my wife, Evalyn, likes to work from prepared recipes, while I like to experiment, sometimes successfully, sometimes not.

As you might expect, cooking and eating are important aspects of the Napa Valley lifestyle. In the wine business, we're constantly entertaining, or being entertained by, friends, customers, and fellow vintners. Despite our hectic business and social schedules, Evalyn and I enjoy cooking for ourselves at home several times a week. In recent years, we've found ourselves lightening these meals, eating less red meat, butter, and sweets and more chicken, fish, and vegetables.

The key to the high quality of wine country cookery is the availability of fresh ingredients. A fabulous cornucopia of fresh fruits and vegetables are available locally, especially in summer. A diverse community is another factor. Napa is home to the descendants of the French, German, and Italian immigrants who settled the valley in the nineteenth century, as well as to many Hispanics. Their culinary legacies are all reflected in the local cuisine, as are Asian influences from nearby San Francisco.

Finally, there's the wine, some of the best in the world. As an ingredient, it adds an accent to a chef's palette of flavors. As an accompaniment, it both complements and enhances the dining experience. On a warm summer day, there's nothing like a rich, crisp Napa Valley Chardonnay with grilled fresh salmon. On a cold winter's night, a fine, complex Cabernet Sauvignon marries perfectly with braised lamb shanks or rabbit stew.

In this book, you will find a diverse sampling of wine country cooking: Trinchero family favorites; seasonal specialties from our two marvelous Sutter Home chefs, Jeffrey Starr and Susanne Salvestrin; and, of course, a cache of delectable dishes from our good friend and America's renowned cookbook master, James McNair. We hope you enjoy them.

If I've learned anything during my sixty-plus years, it's that good food and wine, consumed in moderation with friends and family, makes life all the sweeter. To all of you who will partake of the wonderful food and wine depicted on these pages, *buon appetito!*

—Bob Trinchero
Co-owner and CEO, Sutter Home Winery

sutter home cooking

My congenial association with Sutter Home Winery began on a sun-drenched October weekend in 1990. As an author of a cookbook on grilling, I'd been invited to help judge the winery's first Build a Better Burger national recipe contest. The festivities were held in the beautiful White Zinfandel Garden of the winery's Victorian Inn, located on the outskirts of the charming town of St. Helena, and as I tasted my way through two dozen burgers, I was impressed by the high quality of the contest, the friendly personnel of the winery, and the natural beauty of Napa Valley. Although at that time I'd lived in nearby San Francisco for fifteen years, I'd never spent more than a pleasant day trip in the wine country. During that weekend, I explored the sunny backroads and communities of the valley, and I mused over the possibility of living there someday.

By the time the second annual Build a Better Burger cook-off rolled around the following October, I was in temporary residence at my sister's new home in St. Helena, from which I was launching a daily search for Zeke, my young German shepherd. He had run off into the hills the night we arrived for our first visit with Martha and her family early in September, and during the weeks of intense searching, the appeal of the peaceful valley lifestyle enticed me more each day.

On a crisp autumn day one month after that second cook-off, I moved into my new home overlooking St. Helena and dubbed it "Villa Sunshine." I also recovered Zeke, who'd been living on his own in the hillside vineyard of winemaker Phillip Togni. It seemed that the fates, and my dog, had conspired to lure me here at a time when I needed a sylvan retreat.

Shortly after getting settled, I began my role as culinary spokesperson for Sutter Home, serving as consultant on all food matters and developing recipes to go with their wines. During my years of working with the winery, I've come to admire the dedication of the Trinchero family to making wine accessible to everyone, their commitment to organic farming practices in their vineyards, and their generous contributions to charities and the quality of life for all Napa Valley residents.

When Stan Hock, director of communications for the winery, suggested this cookbook, I eagerly jumped at the chance to put together a collection of recipes from all of the good cooks in the Sutter Home family in a volume that would showcase their approach to the distinctive home cooking of the wine country.

Gathered for a celebration in the White Zinfandel Garden at the Sutter Home Victorian (circa 1884) are the recipe contributors to this book (from left to right): Gina Trinchero Mee, Sutter Home CEO Bob Trinchero, Sutter Home chefs Jeffrey Starr and Susanne Salvestrin, author James McNair, and Evalyn Trinchero.

The Trinchero family has a long history of good cooking, and many of their recipes are scattered throughout this collection of wine-country dishes. Winery founder Mario Trinchero and his wife, Mary, brought their Italian family recipes with them to St. Helena. Since the whole family worked in the winery, they installed a kitchen behind the public tasting room to allow many of the family meals to be prepared and shared there. Mario made most of the antipasti and main dishes, while Mary was the pasta and vegetable expert.

Like his parents, Bob Trinchero, Sutter Home's present CEO, is renowned for his good home cooking. His wife, Evalyn, who was his high-school sweetheart, grew up in a family of hardworking farmers who made cooking a low priority, with the result that meat and potatoes were dinner table mainstays. When Evalyn returned to St. Helena with Bob following his military service, her in-laws happily taught the eager bride to prepare all of their Italian specialties. Even today, Evalyn fondly recalls the frequent celebratory meals shared by the Trinchero family and friends in those early days.

Before their travel schedule as ambassadors for the winery became so hectic, Evalyn and Bob cooked and entertained often, and their home kitchen was designed as two complete kitchens—his and hers—in one room, with separate sinks and cooking stations. They admit to having used lots of cheese and other rich ingredients before health concerns introduced them to the Pritikin dietary principles. While they previously went through gallons of olive oil each year, now just one suffices.

Evalyn and Bob's daughter, Gina Trinchero Mee, who studied enology at the University of California at Davis and holds a degree in Italian literature from Stanford, is currently taking a break from the family business. She enjoys cooking for her family and friends, continuing the longstanding Trinchero tradition of healthy, simple Italian fare. Her contributions to this volume also reflect her interest in current culinary trends.

Sutter Home's in-house chefs, Jeffrey Starr and Susanne Salvestrin, prepare delectable meals for special events at the winery and for overnight guests at the Sutter Home Inn, an elegant Victorian house that dates from 1884. Their innovative recipes selected for this book have been adapted for the home kitchen.

Prior to joining the Sutter Home team, Jeffrey operated his own Napa Valley catering company. He was the first sous chef at Mark Miller's Coyote Cafe in Santa Fe. As executive chef, he created Malibu Adobe with Ali McGraw and others in that southern California beach town.

Like the Trincheros, Susanne Salvestrin's family has lived in Napa Valley for over fifty years. They own a prime vineyard in St. Helena, make their own high-quality Cabernet, and sell the remaining grapes to leading area wineries. A self-taught cook and pastry chef, Susanne prepares breakfasts at the Sutter Home Inn, assists Jeffrey with other meals at the winery, and makes all of the desserts. She also finds time to cook for guests at her family's Sunny Acres Bed and Breakfast Inn in St. Helena and to donate her culinary services to local charities.

I'm also happy to share recipes that I developed in my work for Sutter Home. Some were produced while living under the magical spell of the wine country during my years at Villa Sunshine. Others are recent creations in my San Francisco kitchen that reflect the indelible influences that Napa Valley made upon my culinary style.

Along with the other contributing cooks, I define Napa Valley cooking as a blend of ingredients and techniques brought by valley immigrants from similar sun-drenched winemaking regions of the world. The honest country cooking of France and Italy predominate, with obvious influences from the rest of the Mediterranean. Vineyard workers from Asia and Mexico brought elements of their wonderful cuisines that have also become part of the valley mix. Each wave of settlers adapted the cooking of their homeland to utilize the bounty of California.

The recipes in this book feature the local harvests of the region, including aromatic lavender and rosemary, fresh goat cheese, olives and their fruity oil, wildflower honey, succulent lamb, bushels of Meyer lemons and other just-picked fruits, and, of course, abundant grapes and wonderful wines.

In Napa Valley, wine is not only a featured ingredient in many dishes, but also an important part of the meal. With each recipe, you'll find a wine suggestion, but be sure to read the sidebars on pages 80, 88, 93, and 124 that offer general varietal information and guidelines for pairing wine with food.

Scattered throughout the book are sidebars that share pieces of history, tradition, events, and daily life of the bucolic yet sophisticated Napa Valley. In recent years, the valley has become a Mecca for food professionals and enthusiasts, as evidenced by the arrival of the Culinary Institute of America (see page 83) and the influx of world-class restaurants (see page 55).

Sutter Home proudly offers their wines "for each and every day," a slogan that sums up the attitude of everyone involved in this cookbook. Whether from a highly successful Italian immigrant family, professional chefs, or my own kitchen, the recipes in this collection are offered for your daily enjoyment. Each represents good home cooking, Napa Valley style. It is our wish that they provide you with many pleasures at your own table and invoke the magical valley of the vines.

—James McNair

a short history of wine in the valley

Wine has been made in Napa Valley for 160 years. During the second half of the nineteenth century, the valley was a Mecca for European immigrant vintners, especially those from France, Germany, and Italy, drawn by the valley's beauty, temperate climate, and fertile soils. Pioneers like Charles Krug, Jacob Schram, and Jacob Beringer produced wines celebrated as "bottled poetry" by Robert Louis Stevenson.

The valley's wine business was radically different in those early days. Rarely did wineries age, bottle, or distribute their own products. Those functions instead occurred in large cellars in San Francisco, from which the finished wines were sent by rail or boat to markets across the United States.

This system ended on April 18, 1906, with the great San Francisco earthquake and fire. The area south of Market Street, home to most of the great cellars, was hit hard, and fifteen million gallons of wine were destroyed. In the aftermath,

many wine businesses relocated their cellars to the viticultural regions north of the city, where they unified production, aging, storage, and shipping under a single roof.

Another event that shook the state's wine industry was the passage of the eighteenth amendment to the Constitution, which introduced Prohibition in 1920. Most winemaking ventures were shut down until its repeal in 1933, although some vintners survived by producing sacramental wines.

After repeal, a new generation of growers rushed to join a renascent wine industry. Unfortunately, they often had more energy and enthusiasm than expertise, and the result was a large quantity of inferior wine. Further, the taste for wine had faded among Americans, except for those of European ancestry, and the post-Prohibition wine market remained feeble.

World War II, however, proved kinder to Napa Valley. Because grain products were severely rationed and allocated for food production, the supply of wine exceeded that of beer and spirits. In addition, there was little competition from imports. Americans once again began drinking American wine.

Yet even after the war, there were few wineries in Napa Valley for nearly a quarter century (compared to almost three hundred today). Most were hand-to-mouth operations producing an assortment of generic wines from what today are considered marginal grape varieties. It was not until the wine boom of the 1970s that "noble" varieties such as Chardonnay and Cabernet Sauvignon began to dominate local vineyards.

During the 1970s and 1980s, a new wave of immigrants, this time doctors, lawyers, and businesspeople, flooded the valley eager to begin second lives as winegrowers. Because many of these arrivals dreamed of producing California versions of the great French Bordeaux and Burgundy wines they loved and avidly collected, they energetically planted Cabernet Sauvignon and Chardonnay vines, acquired state-of-the-art equipment and expensive French oak barrels, and recruited skilled winemakers trained at the University of California at Davis School of Viticulture and Enology.

The result was a quantum leap in quality—and prices—for Napa Valley wines, wines that many connoisseurs now consider the equal of the best of France. Today, Napa Valley is acknowledged as America's preeminent wine-growing region, and its wines are regarded as among the finest in the world.

starters

appetizers, soups, and salads

For those occasions when you want a beverage other than a glass of great Napa Valley wine, I've included a refreshing iced wine punch for warm weather and a comforting mulled wine for chilly nights. Either of these complements the easily prepared appetizers featuring wine-country ingredients. Choose a bowl of crunchy walnuts flavored with rosemary, a platter of grape leaves wrapped around creamy goat cheese, or golden fried wontons filled with spicy duck as the prelude to a meal, or prepare an array of nibbles for a wine-tasting party.

Soups are popular throughout the Napa Valley year. Here, you'll find a bright green blend of spring onions and peas, a chilled gazpacho to squelch the blazing summer heat, a roasted corn and chile chowder for crisp autumn days, and a rich, hearty pumpkin porridge to warm up cold-weather evenings. Each soup makes a great little meal on its own or can become an integral part of a special menu.

Likewise, a variety of salads feature seasonal produce and make crisp beginnings to family meals, special lunches, or dinners for friends. You'll also find heartier salads on pages 116 and 117 to enjoy as side dishes during a meal.

vine leaves stuffed with valley goat cheese

SUGGESTED WINE: SAUVIGNON BLANC OR ROSÉ | MAKES **6** SERVINGS

Several wine-country cheese makers produce fine goat cheeses. Choose a creamy, mild cheese to fill grape leaves fresh from the vineyard or commercially preserved. Offer the little packets with wine before dinner or pack them along on a picnic.

INGREDIENTS

About 18 fresh young grape leaves or
    commercial grape leaves packed in brine

3 tablespoons pine nuts or slivered blanched almonds

2 cups crumbled creamy mild goat cheese (about 8 ounces)

2 tablespoons extra-virgin olive oil

$^1/_4$ cup minced mixed fresh herbs such as basil, chives,
    dill, and tarragon

Salt

Freshly ground black pepper

Extra-virgin olive oil for brushing

2 tablespoons freshly squeezed lemon juice

Small clusters of seedless grapes for garnish

If using fresh grape leaves, place a large pan of water over high heat and bring to a boil. Add the leaves and cook until tender, 5 to 15 minutes. Immediately drain the leaves and transfer to a bowl of iced water to halt the cooking. Drain well, pat dry with paper toweling, stack on a plate, and set aside.

If using jarred grape leaves, rinse the leaves under cold running water to remove as much brine as possible. Unfold the leaves, place them in a large pan, and add water to cover. Place over medium heat and bring to a boil, then cover and cook until the leaves are tender, about 25 minutes. Remove the pan from the heat and set aside for the leaves

recipe continues >>

>>

to cool completely in the water. Drain well, pat dry with paper toweling, stack on a plate, and set aside.

In a small skillet, place the pine nuts or almonds over medium heat and toast, shaking the pan or stirring frequently, until lightly golden and fragrant, about 5 minutes. Pour onto a plate to cool and set aside.

In a bowl, combine the goat cheese, the 2 tablespoons oil, and the herbs and beat with a fork until fairly smooth. Season to taste with salt and pepper and stir in the toasted nuts.

Place 1 grape leaf, shiny side down, on a flat work surface. Cut off and discard the tough stem end. Spoon about 1 table-spoon of the cheese mixture in the center near the base of the leaf. Fold the stem end over to cover the filling, then fold both sides inward and tightly roll the leaf toward the pointed tip end to form a compact packet. Place seam side down on a plate. Repeat with the remaining leaves and filling.

Using a pastry brush, lightly coat the rolled leaves with oil, then sprinkle with the lemon juice.

To serve, arrange the leaf packets on a serving platter and garnish with grapes.

Seasons in Napa Valley are measured by the annual growth cycle of the vine. In winter, the vines are in a state of dormancy, reflected in the stark iconography of bare branches shrouded in fog and cloudy, lowering skies.

In mid-March, with warmer days and rain-refreshed soil, green buds poke out from seemingly lifeless wood and slowly, imperceptibly, the vine's foliage begins sketching its canopy. Two months later, flower blossoms appear, heralding the arrival, weeks later, of the hard, tiny infant berries that will grow, with the heat of summer, into heavy, richly colored, juice-laden clusters.

Like the vines, in spring the wine community stirs from its winter hibernation, spent in cellars tending to last year's fledgling wines, traveling the country cultivating new markets, or vacationing in tropical climes. The valley's chefs emerge from their kitchens, where they have been turning out the hearty soups and rib-sticking stews, casseroles, and meats of winter, to explore the season's first blessing of produce, displayed in its glorious bounty in the valley's marketplaces. Soon, there are colorful, inviting salads and pastas, inventive omelets, and the first whiffs of lamb grilling over fragrant firewood.

In spring, too, visitors return to the valley, now awash in sunlit green and vivid mustard, to sample newly bottled White Zinfandels, rosés, and early-maturing whites and, on warmer days, to enjoy the first picnics of the season. Everywhere, the fresh spring air carries reminders of both the cold winter now past and the hot, sun-baked summer days to come.

gorgonzola-stuffed celery

SUGGESTED WINE: SAUVIGNON BLANC | MAKES **12** SERVINGS

Along with prosciutto-wrapped bread sticks, this simple and elegant preparation was a signature appetizer of Sutter Home's founder, Mario Trinchero, who knew his way around a kitchen. Unfortunately, he didn't write down his recipe, but his daughter-in-law, Evalyn, has re-created it here from memory.

When imported Gorgonzola is unavailable, substitute a favorite creamy blue cheese. If you are piping the cheese mixture onto the celery pieces, use a large tip, as the mixture will have little lumps that may block a small opening. The mixture is also good on crisp apple slices.

INGREDIENTS

2 bunches celery

8 ounces Gorgonzola cheese, crumbled

8 ounces cream cheese, at room temperature

2 teaspoons white wine Worcestershire sauce

High-quality Cognac or brandy

Salt

Paprika for garnish

Wash and trim the celery stalks, discarding any that are damaged or discolored. Cut the stalks crosswise into pieces about 3 inches long and pat dry with paper toweling. Set aside.

In the bowl of a stand mixer fitted with a flat beater, combine the cheeses and beat at medium speed until well blended. The mixture will have small lumps. Add the Worcestershire sauce and 1 tablespoon Cognac or brandy and beat well. Add additional Cognac or brandy, a little at a time to taste, and beat until spreadable. Season to taste with salt.

Pipe or spoon the cheese mixture into the celery cavities, then dust lightly with paprika

olive orchard spread

SUGGESTED WINE: SAUVIGNON BLANC | MAKES ABOUT 8 SERVINGS

Tapénade, the intensely flavored olive puree found throughout Provence, is now a Napa Valley staple. It makes a delicious spread for fresh or toasted crusty bread, as well as a tasty topping for baked potatoes, pasta, or pizza. Be sure to use tree-ripened olives that have been cured in brine, not the mildly flavored canned California ripe ones.

INGREDIENTS

1 cup pitted brine-cured ripe olives such as Niçoise

1/2 cup firmly packed fresh basil leaves

1/4 cup olive oil, preferably extra-virgin

3 tablespoons drained small capers

2 tablespoons coarsely chopped garlic

3 flat anchovy fillets packed in olive oil, rinsed and patted dry

1 tablespoon grated or minced fresh lemon zest

2 tablespoons freshly squeezed lemon juice

Freshly ground black pepper

In a food processor, combine all of the ingredients, including pepper to taste, and process until fairly smooth. Transfer to a small bowl, cover, and set aside for up to several hours or refrigerate for up to 2 weeks.

old world bagna cauda *with farmers' market vegetables*

SUGGESTED WINE: ZINFANDEL | MAKES **8** SERVINGS

The Trinchero family has served this traditional Italian appetizer for generations. For dipping, choose a combination of vegetables such as asparagus, broccoli or cauliflower florets, cardoon, celery, cherry tomatoes, fennel, radicchio leaves, summer squash, and sweet peppers. Raw vegetables can be washed, dried, wrapped, and refrigerated for several hours before serving. I prefer to serve most vegetables steamed until crisp-tender, then quickly chilled in iced water to preserve their color. Be sure to drain them well before serving.

INGREDIENTS

About 8 cups raw or steamed vegetables
    (see recipe introduction), trimmed or
    sliced into bite-sized pieces for dipping
$\frac{1}{4}$ cup ($\frac{1}{2}$ stick) unsalted butter
1 tablespoon minced garlic
1 can (2 ounces) flat anchovy fillets packed in olive oil,
    drained and minced
$\frac{3}{4}$ cup extra-virgin olive oil
Crusty Italian bread slices

Prepare the vegetables and reserve as directed in the recipe introduction.

In a heavy saucepan, melt the butter over low heat. Add the garlic and cook, stirring frequently, until soft but not browned, 3 to 4 minutes.

Stir the anchovies into the garlic, then slowly drizzle in the olive oil and blend well. Reduce the heat to keep the mixture barely simmering and cook, stirring frequently, until the oil is well flavored, 10 to 15 minutes; do not allow to brown or burn.

To serve, transfer the hot dip to a heatproof serving dish placed on a warming tray or over an alcohol flame. Arrange the vegetables and bread alongside.

duck wontons with soy-tangerine vinaigrette

SUGGESTED WINE: GEWÜRZTRAMINER | MAKES **8** SERVINGS

Chef Jeffrey Starr sometimes uses ground chicken in place of the duck in the wonton filling. He usually serves the warm wontons around a salad of raw vegetables cut into matchsticks and mixed with some of the Asian-style vinaigrette, but I prefer his tasty wontons on their own as an appetizer or with a simple cabbage slaw tossed with some of his vinaigrette.

INGREDIENTS

2 tablespoons sesame seed

SOY-TANGERINE VINAIGRETTE

2 tablespoons unseasoned rice vinegar

2 tablespoons Dijon mustard

2 tablespoons soy sauce

2 tablespoons brown sugar

1 tablespoon minced fresh ginger

1 tablespoon minced garlic

1 teaspoon crushed dried hot chile

1 tablespoon grated or minced fresh tangerine zest

1 cup freshly squeezed tangerine juice

1 cup Asian sesame oil

WONTON STUFFING

8 ounces ground duck breast

2 tablespoons grated or minced fresh orange zest

2 tablespoons minced unsalted dry-roasted peanuts

1 tablespoon minced fresh cilantro (coriander)

1 tablespoon minced green onion, including green tops

1 tablespoon minced fresh ginger

1 tablespoon minced garlic

1 tablespoon soy sauce

1 tablespoon brown sugar

1$\frac{1}{2}$ teaspoons unseasoned rice vinegar

1 teaspoon crushed dried hot chile

$\frac{1}{2}$ teaspoon ground allspice

$\frac{1}{4}$ teaspoon ground cloves

1 tablespoon Asian sesame oil

Peanut or other high-quality oil for frying

About 24 wonton wrappers

Fresh cilantro (coriander) sprigs for garnish

In a small skillet, place the sesame seed over medium heat and toast, shaking the pan or stirring frequently, until lightly golden and fragrant, about 5 minutes. Pour onto a plate to cool and set aside.

To make the Soy-Tangerine Vinaigrette, in a bowl, combine the vinegar, mustard, soy sauce, sugar, ginger, garlic, chile, and tangerine zest and juice and whisk to blend well. Slowly whisk in the sesame oil. Set aside.

To make the Wonton Stuffing, in a bowl, combine all of the stuffing ingredients and blend well. To test the seasonings, in a small skillet over medium-high heat, cook a small nugget of the mixture until browned. Taste and adjust the seasoning with crushed chile, brown sugar, and soy sauce if necessary to create a good balance of hot, sweet, and salty flavors. Set aside.

Pour oil into a deep fryer or saucepan to a depth of 2 inches and heat to 320 degrees F. Place a wire rack on a baking sheet and set alongside the fryer or stove top. Preheat an oven to 200 degrees F.

Lay 1 wonton wrapper on a work surface. Cover the remaining wrappers with a slightly damp cloth kitchen towel to prevent drying out. Place about 1½ teaspoons of the stuffing mixture in the center of the wrapper. Using a pastry brush, moisten the exposed edges of the wrapper with water, then fold the wrapper over the filling to create a triangle. Pinch the edges together to release as much trapped air as possible. Fill 5 more wonton wrappers in the same way.

Carefully place the 6 wontons in the oil and fry until the bottoms are golden, then turn and fry until the other sides are golden. Using a slotted utensil, transfer the wontons to the rack to drain well, then place the rack and baking sheet in the oven to keep warm until all of the wontons are cooked.

Working with 6 wrappers at a time, fill, seal, fry, and drain the remaining wontons in the same manner, allowing the oil to return to 320 degrees F between batches.

Arrange the warm wontons on a serving platter and drizzle with a little of the reserved vinaigrette. Sprinkle with the toasted sesame seed, garnish with cilantro sprigs, and serve immediately. Place the remaining vinaigrette in a small serving bowl and offer alongside the wontons as a dipping sauce.

grape harvest flat bread

SUGGESTED WINE: PINOT NOIR | MAKES **8** SERVINGS

Americans have come to identify all Italian flat breads or hearth breads, other than pizza, as focaccia, a Ligurian term. Tuscans, however, call their regional flat bread schiacciata, *including this one, which is traditionally made in the Chianti region to celebrate the grape harvest. Since Napa Valley and Chianti are similar in so many ways, it seems appropriate that this slightly sweet bread now makes an appearance in the valley each autumn.*

Enjoy this flat bread with lunch or as an afternoon treat with a glass of wine, but be sure to save some for breakfast.

INGREDIENTS

1/4 cup sugar

2 1/2 teaspoons (1 packet or 1/4 ounce) active dry yeast

3 1/4 cups unbleached all-purpose flour

2 teaspoons salt

1/4 cup olive oil

Olive oil for brushing

3 cups seeded wine grapes or seedless grapes

Sugar for sprinkling, preferably large crystals

In a small bowl, dissolve 1 tablespoon of the sugar in 1 cup warm water (about 110 degrees F). Sprinkle the yeast over the water, stir to dissolve, and let stand until soft and foamy, about 5 minutes. (Discard the mixture and start over with fresh yeast if bubbles have not formed within 10 minutes.)

In the bowl of a heavy-duty stand mixer fitted with a flat beater, combine 3 cups of the flour, the remaining 3 tablespoons sugar, and the salt. Mix at the lowest speed for a few seconds. Add the 1/4 cup oil and the yeast mixture and continue to mix at the same speed for about 1 minute. Replace the flat beater with the dough hook and knead at medium speed until the dough is smooth and elastic, about 5 minutes. Pinch off a piece of dough and feel it. If it is sticky, continue kneading while gradually adding just enough of the remaining 1/4 cup flour for the dough to lose its stickiness. If the dough is dry and crumbly, add warm water, a tablespoon at a time, until the dough is smooth and elastic.

recipe continues >>

>>

Using a pastry brush, generously grease a large bowl with oil. Shape the dough into a ball, place it in the bowl, and turn to coat all over with oil. Cover the bowl tightly with plastic wrap to prevent moisture loss and set aside in a warm, draft-free place for the dough to rise until tripled in bulk, about 2½ hours if using quick-rising yeast, or about 3 hours if using regular yeast.

Meanwhile, to prepare the grapes, preheat an oven to 250 degrees F.

Place the grapes in a single layer in a baking pan, transfer to the oven, and bake just until the grapes are hot and juicy, 15 to 20 minutes; do not allow the grapes to pop open. Transfer the pan to a work surface to cool.

Generously brush a baking sheet with oil. Punch down the dough, then divide it into 2 equal pieces. Form 1 piece into a flat disk and place it in the center of the prepared baking sheet. Using your fingertips, and pulling and stretching with your hands as needed, spread the dough into a round about 12 inches in diameter; it may be springy and a bit difficult to spread. Spoon about one-half of the grapes over the dough, spreading evenly, then press the grapes into the dough with your fingertips. Sprinkle the grapes with about 1 tablespoon sugar.

Form the remaining piece of dough into a disk and place it on a lightly floured work surface. Pull and stretch it into a

12-inch round in the same manner. Place it over the grape-studded dough and press around the edges with your fingertips to adhere the 2 pieces of dough together. Scatter the remaining grapes over the top and press them in gently with your fingertips. Brush the dough all over with oil. Sprinkle generously with sugar. Cover loosely with plastic wrap and set aside to rise until puffy, 30 to 45 minutes if using quick-rising yeast, or 45 minutes to 1 hour if using regular yeast.

Position racks so that the bread will bake in the middle of an oven and preheat the oven to 375 degrees F.

Bake the flat bread until golden brown, 30 to 35 minutes. If the bread puffs up during baking, prick it with a wooden skewer to release air.

Remove the flat bread to a wire rack to cool for about 15 minutes.

Cut into wedges and serve warm or at room temperature.

artichoke leaves with shrimp

SUGGESTED WINE: CHARDONNAY | MAKES **6** SERVINGS

Gina Trinchero Mee, Bob and Evalyn's daughter, created this appetizing combination to serve to guests during the spring artichoke season.

INGREDIENTS

1 medium artichoke

2 bay leaves

1 tablespoon balsamic vinegar

3 ounces cream cheese, at room temperature

1 teaspoon minced garlic

$\frac{1}{4}$ teaspoon hot sauce

Salt

24 small shrimp, cooked, peeled, deveined, and chilled

Paprika for garnish

Cut off the stem of the artichoke flush with the bottom. Then remove the tough outer leaves and cut off the top one-third of the remaining leaves. Place the trimmed artichoke in a saucepan and pour in enough water to cover. Add the bay leaves and vinegar. Place over medium-high heat and bring to a boil, then reduce the heat to achieve a simmer and simmer, uncovered, until the artichoke is tender when pierced with a wooden skewer and the leaves pull away easily, 30 to 45 minutes. (Alternatively, steam the artichoke over boiling water until tender.)

Drain the artichoke and set aside to cool.

When the artichoke is cool enough to handle, remove the firm leaves with edible ends and set aside. You should have about 24 leaves. Discard the soft inner leaves and the fuzzy choke.

Finely chop the artichoke heart and transfer to a bowl. Add the cream cheese, garlic, hot sauce, and salt to taste and blend with a fork until fairly smooth.

To serve, mound about $\frac{1}{2}$ teaspoon of the cheese mixture on the edible end of each reserved artichoke leaf and top with a shrimp. Arrange the leaves on a serving platter and dust the appetizers and the platter lightly with paprika.

rosemary walnuts

SUGGESTED WINE: CABERNET SAUVIGNON OR CHARDONNAY | MAKES **2** CUPS FOR **8** SERVINGS

Rosemary, native to the Mediterranean, grows rampant in the Napa Valley sunshine. Its pungent flavor, somewhat reminiscent of lemon and pine, is perfect on these crispy nuts that are delectable for nibbling with drinks. Although walnut trees from the Prohibition era are still scattered throughout the valley, cashews, pecans, or a mixture of nuts can be substituted for the walnuts.

INGREDIENTS

2 cups walnut halves

1 tablespoon olive oil

2 teaspoons minced fresh rosemary

1 teaspoon salt, or to taste

Preheat an oven to 350 degrees F.

Place the nuts in a shallow baking pan and toast in the oven, stirring frequently, until lightly browned and fragrant, 10 to 15 minutes.

Remove the pan to a work surface. Add the oil, rosemary, and salt and stir until the nuts are well coated. Return to the oven and toast, stirring frequently, until dry, about 5 minutes. Transfer the nuts to a bowl and stir frequently until cool.

mulled winter wine

MAKES **24** SERVINGS

*On a cold winter day in Napa Valley, or elsewhere, a cup of this spiced concoction
is one of my favorite ways to warm up. The mixture can be made ahead and set aside
for up to several hours or covered tightly and refrigerated for up to a week,
then gently reheated in small batches as needed.*

INGREDIENTS

2 bottles (750 ml each) Merlot or Zinfandel

3 cups freshly squeezed orange juice

3 cups pineapple juice

1$^1/_2$ cups freshly squeezed lemon juice

$^3/_4$ cup sugar

36 whole cloves

4 cinnamon sticks

In a nonreactive stockpot, such as stainless steel, combine
all of the ingredients and $^3/_4$ cup water. Place over medium
heat and bring to a simmer. Reduce the heat to very low
and keep warm for about 30 minutes for the flavors to blend.
Strain out the cloves and cinnamon before serving.

To serve, ladle the warm wine into heatproof cups.

summer sangria

SUGGESTED WINE: SAUVIGNON BLANC | MAKES ABOUT **8** SERVINGS

The name of this famous deep red wine punch is derived from the Spanish word for blood. When made with white wine, it becomes sangría blanca. *For an in-between variation, use White Zinfandel or rosé. In any hue, it is the perfect drink for a scorching summer afternoon.*

If you'd like to add a traditional sparkle to the punch, pour in 2 to 3 cups sparkling water or club soda just before serving.

INGREDIENTS

2 bottles (750 ml each) Merlot, Zinfandel, Chardonnay,
    or Chenin Blanc (see recipe introduction)

2 cups freshly squeezed orange or tangerine juice

1/4 cup freshly squeezed lemon or lime juice, or a combination

1/2 cup orange liqueur or brandy, or to taste (optional)

1 orange, thinly sliced

1 lemon, thinly sliced

1 lime, thinly sliced

Sugar (optional)

1/2 cup raspberries or hulled strawberries (optional)

1 cup seedless grapes (optional)

1 cup sliced carambolas (star fruit), nectarines, or peeled
    peaches (optional)

Ice cubes for serving

In a bowl or a pitcher, combine the wine, fruit juices, liqueur or brandy (if using), and citrus slices and stir well. Add a little sugar to taste if the mixture is too tart. Cover tightly and refrigerate until well chilled, at least 3 hours or for up to overnight.

About 30 minutes before serving, stir in the berries, grapes, and carambolas, nectarines, or peaches (if using).

Just before serving, add ice cubes. Pour into wineglasses or tumblers.

spring onion and pea soup

SUGGESTED WINE: CHENIN BLANC OR WHITE ZINFANDEL | MAKES **6** SERVINGS

In spring, wild onions grow rampant in many Napa Valley gardens and meadows. They are the inspiration for this seasonal soup made with their cultivated relatives and tender peas.

If fresh peas are not available, substitute thawed frozen ones. Green garlic, sometimes available in farmers' markets and specialty produce stores and resembling fat green onions, is the young plant harvested before cloves have formed.

INGREDIENTS

3 tablespoons unsalted butter

4 cups sliced leek, including pale green portion

2 cups chopped white or yellow onion, preferably sweet
    varieties such as Maui, Vidalia, or Walla Walla

1 cup chopped green onion, including green tops

2 tablespoons chopped green garlic, including pale
    green portion, or chives

4 cups shelled fresh green (English) peas

6 cups homemade chicken or vegetable stock or canned
    reduced-sodium chicken or vegetable broth

HERBED CREAM

$1/2$ cup heavy (whipping) cream or crème fraîche

Salt

Freshly ground white pepper

2 tablespoons minced fresh herbs such as chervil,
    mint, or tarragon, one type or a mixture

1 tablespoon freshly squeezed lemon juice

Minced fresh chives for garnish

Pesticide-free wild onion, chive, or garlic blossoms
    for garnish (optional)

Stir in the stock or broth and bring to a boil, then reduce the heat to achieve a simmer, cover partially, and simmer until the peas are tender and the flavors are well blended, about 15 minutes.

Remove the pot from the heat and set aside to cool for a few minutes.

Meanwhile, to make the Herbed Cream, in a metal bowl, combine the cream or crème fraîche and a pinch each of salt and pepper. Using a hand mixer or whisk, beat the cream until fairly stiff; avoid overbeating. Stir in the 2 tablespoons herb(s) and refrigerate until serving.

Working in batches, if necessary, transfer the soup to a food processor or blender and puree as smoothly as possible. Press the mixture through a food mill or strainer into a clean pan to remove any stringy pieces. Place over low heat to reheat gently. Just before serving, stir in the lemon juice and season to taste with salt and pepper.

To serve, ladle the soup into warmed bowls. Add a dollop of the Herbed Cream to each serving and sprinkle with chives and blossoms (if using).

In a soup pot, melt the butter over medium-high heat. Add the leek, white or yellow onion, and green onion and cook, stirring frequently, until soft but not browned, about 5 minutes. Add the green garlic or chives and peas and cook for about 2 minutes longer.

summer garden gazpacho

SUGGESTED WINE: SAUVIGNON BLANC | MAKES **6** SERVINGS

Evalyn Trinchero's version of this warm-weather soup features flavorful tomatoes that Bob grows in their flourishing garden overlooking the valley. Be certain to choose vine-ripened tomatoes from your own garden or farmers' market, not the hard, flavorless ones sold in most supermarkets.

INGREDIENTS

8 ripe tomatoes, peeled and seeded

4 cups homemade chicken or vegetable stock or
    canned reduced-sodium chicken or vegetable broth

1 teaspoon minced garlic

1 tablespoon wine vinegar

2 teaspoons sugar

2 teaspoons salt, or to taste

1/4 teaspoon freshly ground black pepper, or to taste

3 drops hot sauce, or to taste

2 cucumbers, peeled, seeded, and finely chopped

1 green sweet pepper, stem, seeds, and membranes discarded,
    then finely chopped

6 radishes, finely chopped

6 green onions, including green tops, finely chopped

Plain nonfat yogurt for garnish

Croutons for garnish

In a food processor or blender, combine the tomatoes, stock or broth, and garlic and blend until fairly smooth. Add the vinegar, sugar, salt, pepper, and hot sauce and blend well. Pour the mixture into a bowl.

Add the cucumbers, sweet pepper, radishes, and green onions and mix well. Cover and refrigerate until well chilled, at least several hours or for up to overnight. Taste the chilled soup and adjust the seasonings before serving.

Ladle the cold soup into chilled bowls, garnish each serving with a dollop of yogurt, and sprinkle with croutons.

summer grilling

In May, when the warmth of summer begins to permeate the valley, the tantalizing aromas of grilling vegetables, fish, poultry, and meats start wafting out from wineries, restaurants, and backyards. Everywhere one spies groups of smiling people, wineglasses in hand, enjoying colorful, alfresco meals featuring the valley's cornucopia of wine and food.

Napa Valley is a paradise for lovers of grilled food. The weather from May through October is warm, dry, and clear. The scenery, with the green, flower-bedecked valley bordered on both sides by mountain ranges, is spectacular. And there's no shortage of wonderful foods to grill and wines to accompany them. Dining and entertaining at home, at wineries, and at restaurants moves outdoors, and all feel blessed to savor the sights, sounds, smells, and tastes of nature in full bloom.

At Sutter Home, the felicitous marriage of grilled food and wine gave birth, in 1990, to the Build a Better Burger contest, a national recipe competition offering a $10,000 Grand Prize to the backyard chef who concocts the most imaginative and appetizing burger. Ingredients of all kinds—vegetables, fish, any kind of meat—are permitted, provided they can be formed into a patty and fit inside a bun or other type of bread.

I've been head judge at the contest since its inception. The climactic annual cook-off is held in early October—arguably the most beautiful time of year in Napa Valley—in the gardens of Sutter Home's majestic Victorian mansion. It is a delightful affair, with talented home cooks from throughout the United States toiling over Weber grills to create a burger that will win the hearts and palates of a judging panel of leading chefs and food writers. Two of the prize-winning burger recipes are included in this book: Portobello Burger (page 102) and Siciliano Burger (page 104).

Burgers and wine? Believe me, there's nothing better than a great burger and a glass of the local Zinfandel or Cabernet to make a gorgeous fall day in Napa Valley even more spectacular!

roasted chile and corn chowder

SUGGESTED WINE: ZINFANDEL | MAKES **6** SERVINGS

*Every Friday morning from late summer through autumn, a smiling vendor at the St. Helena
farmers' market fills a huge wire cylinder with chiles and sweet peppers and rotates it over
glowing coals. I am always intoxicated by the heady aromas that waft from his stand and
find it almost impossible not to buy a few chiles and peppers. Whether purchased from an
outdoor market or prepared at home, roasted chiles and corn add smoky nuances to this
beloved American favorite.*

INGREDIENTS

4 medium-sized ears of corn in husks with ends intact

Vegetable oil for brushing grill rack

3 large Anaheim, New Mexico, poblano, or other
mild to medium-hot chiles

1 tablespoon canola or other high-quality vegetable oil

1 tablespoon unsalted butter

1 cup chopped white or yellow onion

$3/4$ cup finely chopped leek, including pale green portion

About 4 cups homemade chicken or vegetable stock or
canned reduced-sodium chicken or vegetable broth

2 cups finely diced peeled boiling potato (about 1 pound)

$1^1/2$ teaspoons minced fresh thyme, or $1/2$ teaspoon
crumbled dried thyme

1 bay leaf

$1/2$ cup heavy (whipping) cream, light cream, or half-and-half

1 tablespoon minced seeded canned chipotle chile in
adobo sauce, or to taste

Salt

Freshly ground black or white pepper

Adobo sauce from the chipotle chile

Minced fresh chives for garnish

recipe continues >>

>>

Prepare an open grill for moderate direct-heat cooking.

Pull the husks back from the corn, but leave them attached at the base. Remove the silk, then reposition the husks. Tie the narrow end of each ear with a strip of torn husk or cotton string to secure the husks in place. Place in a large bowl, add water to cover, and soak for about 20 minutes, then remove the ears from the water and pat dry with paper toweling.

When the fire is ready, brush the grill rack with vegetable oil. Place the chiles and corn on the rack and grill, turning frequently, until the chiles are blistered and charred all over and the corn is done, 15 to 20 minutes. (Alternatively, roast the chiles over a gas flame or under a broiler and roast the corn in a preheated 375 degree F oven.)

Transfer the chiles to a paper or plastic bag, close the bag loosely, and let stand for about 10 minutes. Transfer the corn to a work surface and let cool.

When the corn is cool, remove the husks. Using a sharp knife, cut the kernels from the cobs into a large bowl and set aside.

Using your fingertips or a small, sharp knife, rub or scrape away the charred skin from the chiles. Cut off and discard the stems. Split the chiles open and scrape out and discard the seeds. Chop the chiles and set aside.

In a soup pot, combine the canola oil and butter and place over medium-high heat. When the butter melts, add the onion and leek and cook, stirring frequently, until the vegetables are soft but not browned, about 5 minutes. Add 4 cups of the stock or broth, the potato, thyme, and bay leaf to the pot and bring the mixture to a boil. Reduce the heat to achieve a simmer, cover, and simmer until the potato is tender when pierced with a wooden skewer or fork, about 15 minutes.

Stir the reserved corn and chopped chile into the soup and simmer for about 3 minutes longer. Stir in the cream and chipotle chile and simmer until heated through, about 5 minutes longer. If the chowder is too thick, add a little more stock or broth. Season to taste with salt, pepper, and a little of the adobo sauce. Remove and discard the bay leaf.

To serve, ladle the soup into warmed bowls, sprinkle with chives, and serve piping hot.

winter squash soup with *toasted pepitas and lime crema*

SUGGESTED WINE: PINOT NOIR | MAKES **6** SERVINGS

Pumpkin patches dot the Napa Valley landscape every autumn. Although this Mexican-inspired soup can be made with flavorful small pumpkins such as Sugar Pie, chef Jeffrey Starr prefers milder relatives of the squash family.

INGREDIENTS

LIME CREMA

¹/₄ cup crème fraîche

1 tablespoon grated or minced fresh lime zest

1 teaspoon freshly ground black pepper

1 teaspoon minced fresh cilantro (coriander)

3 tablespoons unsalted butter

2 pounds Delicata or acorn squash, peeled, seeded, and thinly sliced

1 white or yellow onion, thinly sliced

1 teaspoon minced garlic

1 teaspoon minced fresh serrano or other hot chile

1 tablespoon ground coriander

1 tablespoon ground cumin

3 cups homemade chicken stock or canned reduced-sodium
    chicken broth

1 cup freshly squeezed orange juice

1 tablespoon ground cinnamon

1 tablespoon freshly squeezed lime juice

3 tablespoons minced fresh cilantro (coriander)

Salt

Freshly ground black pepper

¹/₄ cup roasted and salted pumpkin seeds *(pepitas)*

To make the Lime Crema, in a bowl, combine all of the crema ingredients and whisk until smooth. Cover and refrigerate until serving.

In a large saucepan, preferably nonstick, melt the butter over medium heat. Add the squash, onion, garlic, chile, coriander, and cumin. Cook, stirring frequently, until the squash and onion are tender, about 15 minutes.

Add the stock or broth, orange juice, and cinnamon to the squash. Bring to a boil, then reduce the heat to achieve a simmer and simmer for about 2 minutes. Remove from the heat and set aside to cool slightly.

Working in batches if necessary, transfer the soup to a food processor or blender and blend until smooth. Return the soup to a clean pan and place over low heat to reheat gently, then stir in the lime juice, cilantro, salt and pepper to taste.

To serve, ladle the soup into warmed bowls, add dollops of Lime Crema, and sprinkle each serving with the pumpkin seeds.

auction fever

Napa Valley's continuous celebration of food and wine reaches its apogee during the annual Napa Valley Wine Auction, held in early June at the Meadowood Country Club in St. Helena. Inaugurated in 1981, it is the nation's largest charity wine auction, raising several million dollars each year for local hospitals and clinics. The three-day event attracts two thousand wine lovers from throughout the world who bid on rare lots from valley vintners and enjoy a dizzying succession of wonderful culinary events.

On the Thursday afternoon before the auction, an elaborate barrel tasting showcases recent vintage Napa wines paired with an array of valley food specialties. On Friday evening, famed chefs from Napa and beyond collaborate to serve auction attendees an extravagant themed dinner under a vast tent on Meadowood's golf course. Naturally, Napa Valley wines flow throughout the meal.

Saturday's daylong auction evokes scenes from F. Scott Fitzgerald's *The Great Gatsby.* White-suited gentlemen and beautiful women in colorful summer dresses and straw boaters stroll Meadowood's lush greens, sip fine wines, and nibble on creative canapés, while the serious bidders clog the auction tent. The day culminates with a casual alfresco meal following the sale.

During auction week, Sutter Home and other Napa Valley wineries host an assortment of brunches, lunches, and dinners that enable attendees to meet, mingle, and dine with their favorite vintners. Combined with the auction events, these affairs present Napa Valley at its finest, with the region's world-class wine, food, and hospitality taking center stage.

salad of mixed greens *with verjus vinaigrette*

SUGGESTED WINE: SAUVIGNON BLANC | MAKES **8** SERVINGS

Jeffrey Starr uses verjuice—verjus in French—the tart, unfermented juice from grapes, in place of vinegar in his dressing for mixed greens. This staple of medieval kitchens, long out of culinary favor, has experienced a renaissance in recent years. Look for it in specialty gourmet shops and upscale supermarkets. Chef Starr prefers the local Fusion Foods brand made from premium wine grapes.

INGREDIENTS

1 pound mixed small whole or torn tender, young salad greens

VERJUS VINAIGRETTE

2 teaspoons Dijon mustard

1 teaspoon minced shallot

1 teaspoon minced fresh thyme

1 teaspoon minced fresh flat-leaf parsley

1/4 cup verjus

Salt

Freshly ground black pepper

1 tablespoon extra-virgin olive oil

Wash the greens under cold running water. Place in a salad spinner and spin to remove as much water as possible. Pat dry with paper toweling. Wrap in a cloth kitchen towel or paper toweling and refrigerate for at least 30 minutes to crisp, or place the wrapped greens in a plastic bag and refrigerate for up to several hours.

To make the Verjus Vinaigrette, in a small bowl, combine the mustard, shallot, thyme, parsley, verjus, salt and pepper to taste and whisk to blend well. Slowly whisk in the olive oil.

In a bowl, toss the greens with the vinaigrette and serve immediately.

frisée salad with grilled pears, cheese, and walnuts

SUGGESTED WINE: CHARDONNAY OR PINOT NOIR | MAKES **6** SERVINGS

This combination, popular at many Napa Valley restaurants, is one of my favorite special-occasion salads. If frisée, or curly endive, is unavailable, substitute Belgian endive or watercress. In the valley, I used Bartlett pears from my home orchard, but Anjou, Bosc, and Comice varieties all work well. Choose either a mild fresh goat cheese or a high-quality blue cheese such as Gorgonzola, Maytag Blue, Roquefort, or Stilton.

A grill tray, a flat heavy-duty metal tray with a grid of small holes or squares, will keep the pear slices from falling through the grill rack into the fire.

INGREDIENTS

About 8 cups torn frisée

WALNUT VINAIGRETTE

3 tablespoons red wine or sherry vinegar

1 tablespoon minced shallot

2 teaspoons Dijon mustard

1 teaspoon sugar, or to taste

$1/2$ teaspoon salt, or to taste

$1/2$ teaspoon freshly ground black pepper, or to taste

$1/4$ cup walnut oil

$1/2$ cup light olive oil

SWEET CRISPY WALNUTS

1 cup walnut halves

2 tablespoons sugar

Coarse salt

3 ripe but firm pears

Vegetable oil for brushing pears and grill tray

8 ounces creamy blue cheese or mild goat cheese, crumbled

Wash the frisée under cold running water. Place in a salad spinner and spin to remove as much water as possible. Pat dry with paper toweling. Wrap in a cloth kitchen towel or paper toweling and refrigerate for at least 30 minutes to crisp, or place the wrapped greens in a plastic bag and refrigerate for up to several hours.

recipe continues >>

st. helena farmers' market

>>

To make the Walnut Vinaigrette, in a bowl, combine the vinegar, shallot, mustard, sugar, salt, and pepper and whisk to blend well. Slowly whisk in the oils. Set aside.

To make the Sweet Crispy Walnuts, in a skillet, heat the walnuts over low heat, stirring frequently, until they are hot. Sprinkle with the sugar and cook, stirring constantly, until the sugar melts and the nuts are well coated and toasted, about 2 minutes. Watch carefully to prevent burning. Transfer to a bowl, season to taste with coarse salt, and stir frequently until completely cool to keep the walnuts from sticking together. Set aside.

Prepare an open grill for moderate to low direct-heat cooking.

Meanwhile, stem, core, and slice each pear lengthwise into 6 to 8 slices. Using a pastry brush, lightly coat the slices on both sides with vegetable oil.

When the fire is ready, position a grill tray on the grill rack and lightly brush it with oil. Place the pears on the tray and grill, turning once, until heated through, about 2 minutes total cooking time.

To assemble, in a bowl, toss the frisée with just enough of the Walnut Vinaigrette to coat lightly. Mound the frisée on 6 serving plates, dividing equally. Arrange the pear slices over or around the greens, then sprinkle the cheese and the Sweet Crispy Walnuts over the salad. Drizzle the remaining vinaigrette over the pears and cheese and serve immediately.

If you're in Napa Valley on a Friday morning anytime from early May through late October, be sure to pay a visit to the farmers' market in St. Helena (located in Crane Park), the oldest such market in California.

Operated by a local, nonprofit organization, the market features about forty local and regional growers and other vendors. They offer a diverse array of mostly organically grown fruits, vegetables, and flowers, as well as seedlings, fruit trees, baked goods, smoked fish, olive oils, sauces, marinades, and honeys.

It's a colorful, friendly event frequently enlivened by musicians, the works of local artists, and educational programs presented by area chefs and groups such as the California Olive Oil Council. When I lived in the valley, I enjoyed my weekly visits for the camaraderie almost as much as for the bounty, usually lingering with friends and family over coffee and pastries after completing my shopping.

The market is open from the first Friday in May through the last Friday in October, from 7:30 a.m. to 11:30 a.m.

starr caesar salad

SUGGESTED WINE: SAUVIGNON BLANC | MAKES 8 SERVINGS

No volume on Napa Valley cooking could omit the most popular restaurant salad. Jeffrey Starr relies on mayonnaise in place of the traditional coddled egg to add creaminess to the dressing for his rendition of this local favorite.

INGREDIENTS

3 heads romaine lettuce

DRESSING

1/3 cup mayonnaise

1/4 cup freshly grated Parmesan cheese (about 1 ounce),
      preferably Parmigiano-Reggiano

Juice of 1 lemon

1 tablespoon Dijon mustard

1 teaspoon Worcestershire sauce

1 teaspoon prepared horseradish

5 flat anchovy fillets packed in olive oil, rinsed,
      patted dry, and minced

1 teaspoon minced garlic

1/3 cup extra-virgin olive oil

Salt

Freshly ground black pepper

GARNISH

1 cup croutons, preferably made from French bread

Freshly grated Parmesan cheese, preferably Parmigiano-
      Reggiano, for sprinkling

Freshly cracked black pepper

Discard the tough outer leaves from the lettuce. Tear the remaining leaves into large bite-sized pieces, or leave whole for traditional nibbling out of hand. Wash the lettuce under cold running water. Transfer to a salad spinner and spin to remove as much water as possible. Pat dry with paper toweling. Wrap the dried greens in a clean cloth towel or in paper toweling and refrigerate for at least 30 minutes or for up to several hours to crisp.

To make the dressing, in a bowl, combine the mayonnaise, cheese, lemon juice, mustard, Worcestershire sauce, horseradish, anchovies, and garlic and whisk to blend well. Slowly whisk in the olive oil. Season to taste with salt and pepper, cover, and refrigerate for up to several hours.

To assemble, in a bowl, combine the chilled lettuce, croutons, and dressing and toss well. Sprinkle with cheese and cracked pepper to taste and serve immediately.

heirloom tomatoes *with basil, feta, olives, and pine nuts*

SUGGESTED WINE: CHARDONNAY OR ZINFANDEL | MAKES 8 SERVINGS

Late summer and early fall bring an abundance of vine-ripened tomatoes to Napa Valley gardens, roadside stands, and farmers' markets. Choose tomatoes of assorted sizes and colors to create a colorful mosaic for chef Jeffrey Starr's salad platter. I particularly enjoy a combination of heirloom varieties in vivid green, red, yellow, and orange. If desired, scatter tiny whole cherry tomatoes, such as Green Grape or Sweet 100, over the sliced tomatoes. Chef Starr urges the use of the finest-quality olive oil for this preparation.

INGREDIENTS

1/4 cup pine nuts

8 to 12 medium to large ripe tomatoes (see recipe introduction)

6 fresh basil leaves, cut into thin strips (chiffonade)

1/2 cup crumbled feta cheese (about 2 ounces)

1/2 cup chopped pitted Niçoise olives

1/2 cup fruity extra-virgin olive oil

Salt

Freshly cracked black pepper

In a small skillet, place the pine nuts over medium heat and toast, shaking the pan or stirring frequently, until lightly golden and fragrant, about 5 minutes. Pour onto a plate to cool.

Slice the tomatoes and arrange attractively on a serving platter. Sprinkle the basil, cheese, olives, and toasted pine nuts over the tomatoes.

Just before serving, drizzle the olive oil over the tomatoes and sprinkle with salt and pepper to taste.

mustard-marinated leeks

SUGGESTED WINE: SAUVIGNON BLANC | MAKES **4** SERVINGS

Brilliant yellow blankets of wild mustard cover the Napa Valley floor about the time that the first tender leeks appear to herald the end of winter. A sprinkling of those blossoms, which also grow as weeds in many places in and out of the valley, adds a festive note to this salad.

Choose tender, young leeks that are no more than an inch in diameter for this French classic. The leeks can be served as an accompaniment directly from the dish in which they were marinated, or they can be attractively arranged in neat bundles on individual serving plates as a separate salad course. Serve with crusty French bread. If desired, sprinkle a little crumbled crisp bacon over the leeks for added flavor and crunch.

INGREDIENTS

16 thin leeks (1 inch or less in diameter)

1 cup Sauvignon Blanc

1/3 cup white wine vinegar or freshly squeezed lemon juice

1 tablespoon Dijon mustard

1 teaspoon sugar

1/2 teaspoon minced garlic

1/2 teaspoon salt, or to taste

1/2 teaspoon freshly ground black pepper, or to taste

2/3 cup extra-virgin olive oil

Minced fresh chives for garnish

Pesticide-free mustard blossoms for garnish (optional)

Slice off and discard the roots from the leeks, leaving just enough of the root base to hold the leek layers together. Trim the leeks to the same length, discarding the green tops just above the pale green portions. Slice each leek in half lengthwise. Rinse well under cold running water, spreading open the outer layers to be certain that all traces of sand and soil are removed.

Place the leeks in a skillet just large enough to hold them without crowding. Add the wine and enough water to cover the leeks barely. Place over medium-high heat and bring to a simmer, then reduce the heat to maintain a simmer, cover partially, and simmer until the leeks are tender when pierced with a small, sharp knife, 12 to 20 minutes.

Drain the leeks well, then arrange them in parallel rows in a shallow glass or ceramic container.

In a bowl, combine the vinegar or lemon juice, mustard, sugar, garlic, salt, and pepper and whisk to blend well. Slowly whisk in the oil until emulsified. Pour the mixture over the leeks and let stand until the leeks cool to room temperature, at least 1 hour.

Just before serving, sprinkle the leeks with the chives and mustard blossoms (if using).

european influences

Although contemporary Napa Valley cooking draws on a number of ethnic and regional influences, with Asia, Mexico, and the American Southwest among them, Italian and French culinary traditions dominate. This not only reflects the prevalence of French and Italians among the large immigrant populations that helped settle California during the nineteenth century (many of whom became grape growers and winemakers), but also the Mediterranean climate and bountiful produce, including wine, common to the three regions.

Many young California chefs make pilgrimages to France and Italy in search of their culinary muse, and then return to the valley kitchens armed with knowledge ripe for adapting to the local lifestyle. During the 1980s, the cuisine of Italy, especially northern Italy, was ascendant. Restaurants such as Bistro Don Giovanni, Piatti, and Tra Vigne made creative pastas, herb-and-garlic-roasted chicken, and tiramisu standard fare for valley residents, as well as for visitors famished after a day of wine tasting.

In the late 1990s, however, French cooking surged to the forefront of the Napa food scene. Such world-class restaurants as Bistro Jeanty, Bouchon, The French Laundry, and Pinot Blanc brought high-quality French country cuisine to a clientele with both a sophisticated palate and a preference for casual surroundings and hearty, flavorful, full-portioned meals.

Today, visitors to Napa Valley are as likely to come for the food as the wine. Of course, the great appeal of the valley is that you rarely find one without the other.

pasta and risotto

*Like most Americans, Napa Valley diners enjoy pasta and risotto
as a main dish rather than as the traditional Italian intermezzo
between an appetizer and a main course. No matter which way you
choose to serve them, here are a handful of delectable pastas,
a hearty dumpling served like pasta, and a pair of innovative
risottos that capture the flavors of the valley.*

*At the height of the gardening season, be sure to try Evalyn
Trinchero's pasta primavera, abundant with the bounty of valley
harvests. At any time of the year, enjoy Gina Trinchero Mee's
lightened yet seductive version of spaghetti carbonara laced with
roasted garlic. For a special treat, prepare Mary Trinchero's malfatti,
plump dumplings akin to ravioli without the pasta, bathed in the
Trinchero family's version of marinara sauce.*

*Gina offers a light-tasting risotto with spinach and sautéed
scallops, brightened with a squeeze of fresh lemon juice. My
hearty red-wine risotto is rich in color and flavor.*

*With all of these dishes, don't forget a sprinkling of Parmesan
cheese, a loaf of crusty bread, and a bottle or two of
Napa Valley wine.*

evalyn's pasta primavera

SUGGESTED WINE: CHARDONNAY | MAKES 8 FIRST-COURSE OR 4 MAIN-DISH SERVINGS

When preparing the garden-fresh vegetables for this hearty dish, cut each type into bite-sized pieces of roughly the same size. Evalyn Trinchero emphasizes that, because this dish is "twice-cooked," it is important that the vegetables are cooked only until crisp-tender and the spaghetti boiled just until al dente.

INGREDIENTS

$1/3$ cup pine nuts

$1^1/2$ cups sliced asparagus

$1^1/2$ cups sliced green bean

$1^1/2$ cups sliced zucchini

1 cup broccoli florets

$1/2$ cup snow peas or Sugar Snap edible pod peas, stemmed and stringed

$1/2$ cup shelled green (English) peas

1 tablespoon canola or other high-quality vegetable oil

2 cups thinly sliced fresh mushroom

$1/4$ cup finely chopped fresh flat-leaf parsley

$1/2$ teaspoon crushed dried hot chile

6 tablespoons olive oil

4 teaspoons minced garlic

3 cups peeled, seeded, drained, and chopped ripe or canned tomato (reserve juices)

Salt

Freshly ground black pepper

6 large fresh basil leaves

1 pound dried linguine, spaghetti, or other pasta

2 tablespoons unsalted butter

$1/4$ cup homemade chicken stock or canned reduced-sodium chicken broth

$1/2$ cup Chardonnay

$1/4$ cup heavy (whipping) cream

$2/3$ cup freshly grated Parmesan cheese (about $2^2/3$ ounces), preferably Parmigiano-Reggiano

In a small skillet, place the pine nuts over medium heat and toast, shaking the pan or stirring frequently, until lightly golden and fragrant, about 5 minutes. Pour onto a plate to cool and set aside.

Bring a pot of water to a boil over high heat and ready a bowl of iced water.

When the water boils, add the asparagus and cook until crisp-tender. Using a slotted utensil, quickly remove the asparagus to the iced water. Return the pot of water to a boil, then separately cook and chill the green bean, zucchini, broccoli, pod peas, and shelled peas in the same manner, allowing the pot of water to return to a boil each time before adding the next vegetable. Cooking time will vary with each vegetable, from about 1 minute for the peas to about 5 minutes for the broccoli.

When all of the vegetables are cooked and cooled, drain them well and set aside.

In a large skillet or sauté pan, heat the vegetable oil over medium-high heat. Add the mushroom and cook, stirring frequently, until tender, about 2 minutes. Stir in the chopped parsley and chile, transfer to a bowl, and set aside.

In the same skillet, heat 3 tablespoons of the olive oil over medium heat. Add 2 teaspoons of the garlic, the tomato (reserve the juices), salt and pepper to taste. Cook, stirring frequently, for about 5 minutes. Tear the basil into small pieces, stir into the mixture, transfer to a bowl, and set aside.

In a large pot, bring 4 quarts water to a rapid boil over high heat. When the water boils, stir in 1 tablespoon salt. Drop the pasta into the boiling water and cook, stirring frequently, until tender but still firm to the bite.

Meanwhile, in the skillet, heat the remaining 3 tablespoons olive oil over medium-low heat. Add the remaining 2 teaspoons garlic and cook, stirring frequently, until soft, about 2 minutes. Add the blanched vegetables, reduce the heat to low, and stir just until heated through.

Drain the pasta well and set aside.

In the pot used for cooking the pasta, melt the butter over low heat. Add the stock or broth, wine, cream, and cheese and stir constantly until the mixture is smooth and creamy. Add the drained pasta and toss quickly to coat. Add half of the vegetable mixture and the reserved tomato juices and continue to toss and stir the mixture over low heat. Stir in the remaining vegetable mixture, the reserved mushroom mixture, the toasted pine nuts, and salt and pepper to taste.

To serve, reheat the reserved tomato mixture. Divide the pasta among warmed shallow bistro bowls, top with equal portions of the tomato mixture, and serve immediately.

PENNE WITH ROASTED EGGPLANT AND PEPPER | PASTA AND RISOTTO

penne with roasted eggplant and pepper

SUGGESTED WINE: MERLOT OR ZINFANDEL | MAKES 8 FIRST-COURSE OR 4 MAIN-DISH SERVINGS

The sunny flavors in this combination are a reminder of the Mediterranean homelands of many Napa Valley residents.

INGREDIENTS

2 medium-sized globe eggplants, peeled if desired, cut into 1-inch cubes

2 red onions, sliced vertically into thin strips

3 red sweet peppers, stems, seeds, and membranes discarded, then cut into narrow strips

$1/4$ cup olive oil

2 teaspoons minced garlic

1 tablespoon minced fresh rosemary, or 1 teaspoon crumbled dried rosemary

$1^1/2$ teaspoons minced fresh oregano, or $1/2$ teaspoon crumbled dried oregano

Salt

Freshly ground black pepper

$1/4$ cup pine nuts

1 pound penne or other dried short tubular pasta

1 cup chopped or shredded fresh basil

1 cup crumbled mild goat or feta cheese (about 4 ounces)

Preheat an oven to 375 degrees F.

In a roasting pan or other large baking pan, combine the eggplants, onions, and peppers. Add the oil, garlic, rosemary, oregano, and generous sprinklings of salt and pepper. Stir the vegetables in the seasonings to coat. Transfer to the oven and roast, stirring every 10 minutes, until the eggplant is very tender when pierced with a wooden skewer or fork, 35 to 45 minutes.

In a small skillet, place the pine nuts over medium heat and toast, shaking the pan or stirring frequently, until lightly golden and fragrant, about 5 minutes. Pour onto a plate to cool and set aside.

In a large pot, bring 4 quarts water to a rapid boil over high heat. When the water boils, stir in 1 tablespoon salt. Drop the pasta into the boiling water and cook, stirring frequently, until tender but still firm to the bite.

Drain the pasta in a colander. Rinse the pasta pot and return it to the stove over the lowest heat. Add the drained pasta and the roasted vegetables, stirring to mix thoroughly and to heat through. Stir in the toasted pine nuts and the basil.

Divide the pasta among warmed serving plates or shallow bistro bowls, sprinkle with the cheese, and serve immediately.

spaghetti carbonara *with roasted garlic*

SUGGESTED WINE: MERLOT | MAKES **4** FIRST-COURSE OR **2** MAIN-DISH SERVINGS

Gina Trinchero Mee's use of creamy sweet roasted garlic and American-style bacon adds a contemporary Napa Valley touch to this beloved Roman preparation.

INGREDIENTS

4 to 6 garlic cloves, peeled

2 tablespoons unsalted butter, at room temperature

Salt

$1/2$ pound dried spaghetti

$1/2$ pound sliced bacon

2 eggs, at room temperature, lightly beaten

$1/4$ cup light cream or half-and-half

$1/3$ cup freshly grated Parmesan cheese (about 1$1/3$ ounces),
      preferably Parmigiano-Reggiano, plus extra for passing

Freshly cracked black pepper

Preheat an oven to 350 degrees F.

Wrap the garlic cloves in aluminum foil to form a packet. Roast in the oven until soft and golden brown, about 30 minutes.

Unwrap the garlic and transfer to a small bowl. Add the butter and mash with a fork. Set aside.

In a large pot, bring 4 quarts water to a rapid boil over high heat. When the water boils, stir in 1 tablespoon salt. Drop the spaghetti into the boiling water and cook, stirring frequently, until tender but still firm to the bite.

Meanwhile, in a skillet, cook the bacon over medium heat until crisp. Transfer to paper toweling to drain well, then crumble and set aside.

In a small bowl, combine the eggs and cream and whisk to blend well. Set aside.

Drain the spaghetti in a colander. Rinse the pasta pot and return it to the stove over the lowest heat. Add the roasted garlic mixture, swirl to coat the bottom of the pot, add the drained spaghetti, and immediately toss to coat well.

Remove from the heat, add the egg mixture to the hot spaghetti, and stir constantly until it has thickened and formed a sauce. Add the crumbled bacon, the $1/3$ cup cheese, and salt and pepper to taste, and toss to coat thoroughly.

Transfer the spaghetti to a warmed serving dish or divide it among warmed serving plates or shallow bistro bowls and serve immediately. Pass additional cheese and pepper at the table.

malfatti with mushroom marinara sauce

SUGGESTED WINE: ZINFANDEL | MAKES **8** SERVINGS

After moving to Napa Valley with her husband, Mario, and children, Mary Trinchero worked ten-hour days on the winery bottling line, kept the books, and cooked family meals, including malfatti, in the kitchen behind the tasting room.

In spite of my culinary research in Italy and writing two books on Italian cooking and two books on pasta, I'd never encountered malfatti until moving to Napa Valley. My good friend Antonia Allegra, then editor of Appellation magazine, took me to the venerable American-Italian restaurant The Depot, in the city of Napa, for the house specialty, malfatti, which she describes as "ravioli without the pasta casing." This true comfort food is so popular with longtime valley residents that people arrive at the kitchen door of The Depot with empty pots and casseroles to be filled with malfatti for at-home family dining and entertaining.

Malfatti, which loosely translates as "badly made," have a rustic appearance. Various mixtures of meat and vegetables, often leftovers, are bound together, shaped and cooked like dumplings, and served with a simple cheese sauce, often made with Gorgonzola, or a flavorful tomato sauce.

INGREDIENTS

MUSHROOM MARINARA SAUCE (PAGE 66)

MALFATTI

1 tablespoon olive oil

1 tablespoon unsalted butter

1 teaspoon minced garlic

$1/2$ cup chopped fresh flat-leaf parsley

1 tablespoon minced fresh rosemary, or
    1 teaspoon crumbled dried rosemary

Pinch of dried oregano

3 pounds fresh Swiss chard, or 3 packages (10 ounces each)
    frozen Swiss chard, thawed

1 pound ground lean beef

1 loaf (about 1 pound) day-old French bread, torn into pieces

5 eggs, lightly beaten

1 cup freshly grated Parmesan cheese (about 4 ounces),
    preferably Parmigiano-Reggiano, plus extra for serving

2 cups all-purpose flour, plus extra for dusting

Salt

Freshly ground black pepper

Prepare the Mushroom Marinara Sauce as directed and set aside.

To make the malfatti, in a skillet, combine the oil and butter and place over medium heat. When the butter is melted, add the garlic, parsley, rosemary, and oregano and cook, stirring frequently, for 5 minutes. Remove from the heat and set aside to cool slightly.

If using fresh chard, discard the tough stems and wash the leaves well. Transfer the damp chard to a sauté pan or heavy skillet, place over high heat, and cook, stirring frequently, until the chard wilts and turns bright green, about 5 minutes.

Place the freshly cooked or thawed chard in a colander to drain, then gently squeeze to release as much moisture as possible. Transfer the chard to a bowl, add the ground beef, bread, and the cooled garlic mixture, and stir to mix well.

Place the mixture in a food processor and process finely, then transfer to a large bowl. (Alternatively, grind the mixture through a meat grinder into a large bowl.) Add the eggs, the 1 cup cheese, the 2 cups flour, salt and pepper to taste and mix thoroughly to form a stiff dough.

Dust a baking sheet lightly with flour and set aside. Using an oval spoon, form the meat mixture into ovals about 1½ inches long; for smoother dumplings, lightly dust your hands with flour and roll each piece between your palms, then shape with your fingertips. Roll each oval in flour and place on the prepared baking sheet. (At this point the baking sheet can be placed in a freezer until the malfatti are hard, about 2 hours, then transfer the dumplings to airtight freezer bags and freeze for up to 2 months. Cook the malfatti while still frozen, allowing a little extra time.)

In a large pot, bring 4 quarts water to a rapid boil over high heat, then stir in 1 tablespoon salt. Preheat an oven to 200 degrees F.

Drop about 15 malfatti into the boiling water (avoid crowding) and boil until they rise to the surface, then cook 1 to 2 minutes longer. To test for doneness, cut into a malfatti and taste to be certain it is no longer gummy. Using a slotted utensil, transfer to a colander to drain well, then transfer to a large, shallow ovenproof platter and place in the oven to keep warm. Cook and drain the remaining malfatti in the same manner.

Meanwhile, reheat the Mushroom Marinara Sauce.

To serve, toss the malfatti with the sauce and sprinkle with cheese.

mushroom marinara sauce

SUGGESTED WINE: CHARDONNAY OR ZINFANDEL | MAKES ABOUT 4 CUPS FOR 8 SERVINGS

Simple, zesty marinara originated with Italian sailors as a quick sauce to serve with pasta and the catch of the day. Evalyn Trinchero adds mushrooms to the Old World sauce and emphasizes that it must not be cooked too long once the fresh herbs are added, as they should retain heir fresh green color. Evalyn recommends using everyday cultivated white mushrooms or their darker cremino relatives. For a more robust flavor, the sauce can be made with porcino, shiitake, or other flavorful mushrooms.

Serve the sauce with malfatti (see page 64) or your favorite cooked pasta. And don't forget to offer plenty of freshly grated Parmesan cheese for adding at the table.

INGREDIENTS

1 1/2 tablespoons olive oil

2 teaspoons minced garlic

2 cups peeled, seeded, drained, and chopped ripe
    or unsalted canned tomato

1 1/2 cups pureed ripe or canned tomato or reduced-sodium
    tomato sauce

1 cup Chardonnay

8 ounces fresh mushrooms, thinly sliced or finely chopped

1/3 cup lightly packed torn fresh basil leaves

1/3 cup chopped fresh flat-leaf parsley

Crushed dried hot chile

Salt

Freshly ground black pepper

In a skillet, heat the oil over medium heat. Add the garlic and cook, stirring frequently, until soft and golden, about 5 minutes. Add the chopped tomato, pureed tomato or tomato sauce, wine, and mushrooms. Bring to a simmer, then adjust the heat to maintain a simmer and cook for 15 minutes.

Stir the basil and parsley into the simmering sauce. Season generously with chile, salt, and pepper to taste. Continue to simmer for about 10 minutes longer; do not overcook.

Use as directed in recipes.

spinach risotto with sautéed scallops

SUGGESTED WINE: SAUVIGNON BLANC OR CHARDONNAY | MAKES 8 FIRST-COURSE OR 4 MAIN-DISH SERVINGS

Gina Trinchero Mee created this light yet satisfying risotto, perfect for warm-weather dining. Gina prefers tiny bay scallops, which are more succulent than larger sea scallops, for this preparation. Be sure to purchase fresh, sweet-smelling scallops and be careful not to overcook them.

INGREDIENTS

4 cups packed spinach leaves, washed and drained

About 6 cups light homemade chicken stock, or 3 cups canned reduced-sodium chicken broth diluted with 3 cups water

1 tablespoon olive oil

1 teaspoon minced garlic

1 1/2 cups Italian Arborio, Carnaroli, or Vialone Nano rice

1/2 cup chopped yellow or white onion

3/4 cup Sauvignon Blanc or Chardonnay

1/4 teaspoon salt

1/4 teaspoon freshly ground black pepper

1 tablespoon unsalted butter

12 ounces bay scallops, rinsed and drained

Lemon wedges for serving

If using tender baby spinach, set whole leaves aside. If using large spinach, discard the stems, tear the leaves into pieces, and set aside.

In a saucepan, bring the stock or diluted broth to a simmer over high heat, then reduce the heat to maintain a simmer while cooking the rice.

In a heavy, deep sauté pan or skillet, heat the oil over medium heat. Add the garlic and cook, stirring frequently, until lightly browned, about 3 minutes. Using a slotted spoon, remove the browned garlic to a plate and set aside for later use.

Add the rice and onion to the pan, reduce the heat to medium-low, and cook, stirring frequently, for about 5 minutes; the mixture will get very dry. Add 1/2 cup of the wine, the salt, and pepper and stir constantly until the wine has been absorbed, less than 1 minute.

recipe continues >>

SPINACH RISOTTO WITH SAUTEÉD SCALLOPS | PASTA AND RISOTTO

Add ½ cup of the simmering stock or broth, adjusting the heat under the rice if the liquid is evaporating too quickly. Keep the rice at a simmer and stir almost continuously, scraping the bottom and sides of the pan, until the liquid has been absorbed.

Continue to add the warm stock or broth ½ cup at a time each time the rice becomes dry, and continue to stir the rice as it cooks. As the risotto approaches completion, add the stock or broth only ¼ cup at a time. The rice may be done before all the liquid is added, or you may need more liquid, in which case add more stock or broth or hot water. Cook until the rice is tender but firm to the bite, about 25 minutes in all. Completed risotto should be creamy but not soupy. If it is too dry, add a little more stock, broth, or hot water.

When the rice is done, stir in the reserved garlic and spinach, cover, remove from the heat, and set aside while you cook the scallops; the residual heat will wilt the spinach.

In a skillet, melt the butter over medium heat. Add the scallops and cook, turning several times, just until no longer translucent, 2 to 3 minutes. Add the remaining ¼ cup wine and cook, stirring, for about 1 minute longer.

To serve, scoop the risotto onto warmed plates and spread slightly. Top with the scallops and garnish each serving with lemon wedges for squeezing at the table.

entertaining in the valley

In Napa Valley, matching wine with food, and vice-versa, is a favorite pastime, not only as a pleasurable pursuit in itself, but also as an important way for wineries to promote their products.

Of the nearly three hundred wineries in Napa Valley, most are small, family-owned operations. Even the smallest of them entertain regularly, however, meaning they have an in-house chef, a frequently employed caterer, or a proprietor with accomplished cooking skills. Lunches and dinners at wineries, or at the valley's fine restaurants, to entertain distributors, retailers, restaurateurs, wine writers, and fellow vintners, are regular occurrences. In Napa Valley, eating and drinking well, in surroundings of casual elegance, are both a lifestyle and the lifeblood of wine commerce.

At Sutter Home, for example, chefs Jeffrey Starr and Susanne Salvestrin start the day making baked goods for breakfasters staying at the Sutter Home Inn. They may then create an elegant three-course lunch for a small group of VIPs and winery executives, prepare a late-afternoon barbecue for fifty visiting distributors, and cook a formal dinner for the Trincheros and selected guests. The kitchen hums with activity from dawn to late evening, as Jeffrey, Susanne, and their helpers prep, cook, serve, bus, and clean. At all times, quality, hospitality, and professionalism are foremost.

In Napa Valley, a place mixing California chic with timeless agrarian rhythms, the fabulously rich with toiling farm workers, old valley families with urban arrivistes, meals are an occasion to conduct business, entertain friends, and to enjoy and celebrate the bounty of a provident nature.

red-wine risotto *with olives and sun-dried tomatoes*

SUGGESTED WINE: MERLOT OR ZINFANDEL | MAKES 8 FIRST-COURSE OR 4 MAIN-DISH SERVINGS

The array of superb olives at Oakville Grocery and Dean & DeLuca in St. Helena inspired this simple risotto that is delicious with grilled lamb or other meats. Choose high-quality green or black olives, or a mixture, packed in brine or olive oil.

INGREDIENTS

About 5 cups homemade chicken or vegetable stock or canned
    reduced-sodium chicken or vegetable broth

2 tablespoons olive oil

$1/2$ cup finely chopped shallot or red onion

1 teaspoon minced garlic

$1^1/2$ cups Italian Arborio, Carnaroli, or Vialone Nano rice

$1^1/2$ cups Merlot or Zinfandel

$1/2$ cup chopped pitted olives (see recipe introduction)

$1/2$ cup chopped drained sun-dried tomatoes packed in olive oil

$1/2$ cup freshly grated Parmesan cheese (about 2 ounces),
    preferably Parmigiano-Reggiano, plus extra for sprinkling

Salt

Freshly ground black pepper

In a saucepan, bring the stock or broth to a simmer over high heat, then reduce the heat to maintain a simmer while cooking the rice.

In a heavy, deep sauté pan or skillet, heat the oil over medium-high heat. Add the shallot or onion and cook, stirring frequently, until soft but not browned, about 5 minutes. Add the garlic and rice and stir until all of the grains are well coated, about 2 minutes. Add $1/2$ cup of the wine and cook, stirring constantly, until the wine has evaporated, about 3 minutes. Add the olives, tomatoes, and $1/2$ cup of the remaining wine, adjusting the heat under the rice if the liquid is evaporating too quickly. Keep the rice at a simmer and stir almost continuously, scraping the bottom and sides of the pan, until the liquid has been absorbed.

Continue to add the wine, then the simmering stock or broth $1/2$ cup at a time each time the rice becomes dry, and continue to stir the rice as it cooks. As the risotto approaches completion, add the stock or broth only $1/4$ cup at a time. The rice may be done before all the liquid is added, or you may need more liquid, in which case add more stock or broth or hot water. Cook until the rice is tender but firm to the bite, about 25 minutes in all.

When the rice is done, add the $1/2$ cup cheese and stir for about 2 minutes. Completed risotto should be creamy but not soupy. If it is too dry, add a little more stock, broth, or hot water. Season to taste with salt and pepper.

To serve, spoon onto warmed plates and sprinkle lightly with cheese. Pass additional cheese at the table for sprinkling over individual servings.

main dishes and accompaniments

Napa Valley home chefs love to cook outdoors from spring through fall, or even on warm winter days, when grilled fare plays the starring role at lunch or dinner. In this section, you'll find recipes for grilling salmon, chicken, lamb, burgers, and vegetables, each accompanied with flavorful condiments and sauces.

For indoor cooking at any time of the year, you'll find delectable main-dish preparations for sautéing shrimp, roasting chicken and beef, stewing chicken, and braising lamb shanks. Wine is an important component of many of these dishes, as well as the perfect beverage to accompany them. Also keep in mind that the pastas and risottos in the preceding chapter make great main dishes.

Some of my favorite recipes in this section are for side dishes of vegetables, grains, and salads. A few are so hearty that they can be also be served as vegetarian main dishes, or you can make two or three of them to combine for a memorable meatless meal.

grilled fillet of salmon with *mango-chipotle salsa*

SUGGESTED WINE: SAUVIGNON BLANC, WHITE ZINFANDEL, OR DRY ROSÉ | MAKES 6 SERVINGS

Napa Valley cooks like to prepare the fresh salmon caught by fishermen from nearby San Francisco. This simple dish features a fiery fruit salsa inspired by the cooking of Hispanic residents of the valley.

Sutter Home chef Jeffrey Starr warns that the grill rack must be well seasoned and very hot before putting the salmon on it. He advises never to wash the rack between uses. Instead he says to scrape it with a wire brush while it is still hot after cooking, and to oil it generously when hot just before putting the fish on it. In time the rack will develop a nonstick, well-seasoned surface. The fish can also be grilled in a greased hinged grill basket for easier turning, or it can be cooked under a hot broiler on an oven rack at the highest position.

If made in late summer or early fall when tomatoes are at their peak, the salsa tastes great with the addition of chopped tomato or whole very small tomatoes, such as Sweet 100 or Currant tomatoes.

INGREDIENTS

MANGO-CHIPOTLE SALSA

2 ripe but firm mangoes, peeled, pitted, and cut into $1/2$-inch cubes

1 ripe but firm avocado, peeled, pitted, and cut into $1/2$-inch cubes

$1/2$ cup chopped red sweet pepper

$1/4$ cup chopped red onion

40 fresh cilantro (coriander) leaves

3 tablespoons unseasoned rice vinegar

1 tablespoon light brown sugar

3 to 6 canned chipotle chiles packed in adobo sauce, rinsed, seeded, and finely minced

$1/2$ teaspoon salt

1 whole salmon fillet (about $2^1/2$ pounds), with skin intact

3 tablespoons olive oil for brushing

Salt

Freshly ground black pepper

Vegetable oil for brushing grill rack

To make the Mango-Chipotle Salsa, in a bowl, combine all of the salsa ingredients and stir to mix well. Cover and refrigerate for at least 1 hour or for up to several hours.

Prepare an open grill for hot direct-heat cooking.

Brush the salmon all over with the olive oil and sprinkle with salt and pepper to taste.

When the fire is ready, generously brush the grill rack with vegetable oil. Place the salmon, flesh side down, on the grill. Grill for about 3 minutes, then turn and cook, skin side down, just until the flesh is opaque when cut into at the thickest part with a small, sharp knife, about 3 minutes longer, or a total of about 10 minutes per inch of thickness; avoid overcooking.

Transfer the fish, flesh side up, to a warmed serving platter and top with the salsa.

SAUTÉED SHRIMP WITH PEPPERS AND FETA | MAIN DISHES AND ACCOMPANIMENTS

sautéed shrimp with peppers and feta

SUGGESTED WINE: SAUVIGNON BLANC | MAKES 4 SERVINGS

Here's another recipe from Gina Trinchero Mee that features Mediterranean ingredients and reflects the lighter cooking style of her family. Serve the shrimp with rice or couscous.

INGREDIENTS

2 teaspoons olive oil

2 teaspoons minced garlic

1 red sweet pepper, stem, seeds, and membranes discarded, then sliced into narrow strips

1 green sweet pepper, stem, seeds, and membranes discarded, then sliced into narrow strips

1 pound large shrimp, peeled and deveined

2 tablespoons freshly squeezed lemon juice

2 tablespoons chopped fresh flat-leaf parsley

1 teaspoon fresh thyme leaves, or $1/2$ teaspoon crumbled dried thyme

$1/2$ cup crumbled feta cheese

$1/4$ teaspoon freshly cracked black pepper

Salt

In a large skillet or sauté pan, heat the oil over medium heat. Add the garlic and cook, stirring frequently, for 1 minute. Add the sweet peppers and continue cooking and stirring until the peppers are soft but not browned, about 15 minutes.

Add the shrimp, lemon juice, parsley, and thyme to the pan and cook, stirring frequently, until the shrimp turn bright pink and opaque, about 4 minutes. Sprinkle with the cheese, black pepper, and salt to taste. Cover, remove from the heat, and let stand until the cheese softens slightly, about 1 minute.

Serve immediately.

grilled raspberry chicken breasts

SUGGESTED WINE: MERLOT, PINOT NOIR, OR WHITE ZINFANDEL | MAKES **6** SERVINGS

*Raspberries are a staple of Napa Valley markets. When combined with red wine and good
mustard, they add a distinctive flavor to chicken breasts.*

INGREDIENTS

MARINADE

$3/4$ cup pureed fresh or thawed frozen unsweetened raspberries

$1/4$ cup Merlot or Pinot Noir

$1/4$ cup red wine vinegar, preferably raspberry flavored

$1/4$ cup olive oil, preferably extra-virgin

2 tablespoons Dijon mustard

2 tablespoons minced fresh mint

1 tablespoon minced garlic

2 teaspoons grated or minced fresh lime or lemon zest

$1/2$ teaspoon salt, or to taste

$1/4$ teaspoon freshly ground black pepper, or to taste

6 boned and skinned chicken breast halves

Vegetable oil for brushing grill rack

Fresh raspberries for garnish (optional)

Chopped fresh mint for garnish

Thin fresh lime or lemon slices for garnish

In a nonreactive (glass, stainless steel, or ceramic) bowl, combine all of the marinade ingredients, stir well, and set aside.

Quickly rinse the chicken under cold running water and pat dry with paper toweling. Place the chicken in the marinade and turn to coat all sides of the chicken. Cover and let stand, turning occasionally, at room temperature for about 2 hours, or refrigerate for up to overnight (return the chicken to room temperature before grilling).

Prepare an open grill for moderate direct-heat cooking.

Remove the chicken from the marinade and set aside. Pour the marinade into a saucepan and bring to a boil over medium-high heat, then set alongside the grill.

When the fire is ready, lightly brush the grill rack with vegetable oil. Place the chicken on the rack and grill about 5 minutes. Turn the chicken and continue grilling, brushing occasionally with the marinade, until the chicken is opaque but still moist inside when tested by cutting with a small sharp knife at the thickest point, 8 to 10 minutes' total cooking time.

Serve hot or at room temperature. If desired, return any remaining marinade to a boil and serve with the chicken. Garnish with fresh berries (if using), chopped mint, and lemon or lime slices.

pairing food and wine

The days of politically correct wine and food pairings—no red wine with fish or white wine with meat—are, thankfully, over. Today's less rigid approach, long espoused by the Trincheros at Sutter Home, is to drink the wines you like with the foods you like. Nonetheless, a few basic guidelines can help maximize your enjoyment of food and wine.

Matching flavor intensities and textures is the best way to create great food-wine matches. For example, with a lean, mildly flavored dish like roasted chicken, a crisp, mildly flavored white, like a Sauvignon Blanc or lighter Chardonnay, is preferable to a big, buttery Chardonnay or a rich, full-bodied red. A light red Beaujolais, Chianti, or Pinot Noir would work, too. Remember that the dominant flavor of the food may not come from the main ingredient, but from its sauce or seasoning. Therefore, if that same roasted chicken is plunged into a rich cream sauce, the buttery Chardonnay becomes a better choice. Similarly, if you serve a white or light red with chili, you probably will taste only the chili. But pour a hearty, spicy Zinfandel with the chili and you will have a great match.

High-acid foods like sauerkraut, sweet-and-sour sauces, and oil-and-vinegar salad dressings are anathema to a bold Chardonnay, a plump Merlot, or other full-bodied wines that lack sufficient acidity of their own. Such acidic foods instead should be paired with high-acid wines such as Sauvignon Blanc or Barbera.

Fatty foods normally call for wines with lots of body, glycerine, and flavor. Beef or game, for example, needs a full-bodied red like Cabernet Sauvignon. Fried foods, however, often work better with leaner, more acidic wines, which tend to cut the grease in the food.

Sometimes the most successful pairings come from contrasting the flavors of the food and the wine in a way that elevates both. The best example is pairing strongly flavored, spicy Indian, Thai, or Mexican cuisine with light-bodied, slightly sweet wines such as White Zinfandel, Riesling, Gewürztraminer, or Chenin Blanc. Whereas a drier, more alcoholic wine might ignite the heat in these dishes, the lighter, fruitier wines both frame and tame their spiciness.

honey, mustard, and rosemary pan-roasted chicken *with chardonnay sauce*

SUGGESTED WINE: SAUVIGNON BLANC | MAKES ABOUT 8 SERVINGS

Here, rosemary, prolific throughout Napa Valley, teams with mustard and honey to infuse chicken. Boned pieces cook quickly with this method, which results in succulent flesh and crispy skin. Use the same technique for halved poussins or other small chickens; cooking time will vary with size and thickness of the birds. To cook more servings, use additional skillets.

The simple wine sauce is also wonderful with grilled or panfried steaks or pork tenderloins; substitute beef stock or broth for the chicken stock or broth and Cabernet Sauvignon or Zinfandel for the Chardonnay.

INGREDIENTS

8 boned chicken breast halves or thighs with skin intact, or a combination

Salt

Freshly ground black pepper

1/4 cup olive oil

2 tablespoons Dijon mustard

1 tablespoon honey

1 tablespoon minced fresh rosemary, or 1 teaspoon crumbled dried rosemary

1/2 teaspoon ground cayenne or other dried hot chile, or to taste

CHARDONNAY SAUCE

2 cups homemade chicken stock or canned reduced-sodium chicken broth

1 cup Chardonnay

1 teaspoon green peppercorns packed in brine, drained and crushed (optional)

2 teaspoons cornstarch

Salt

Freshly ground black pepper (if not using green peppercorns)

Fresh rosemary sprigs for garnish

recipe continues >>

>>

Quickly rinse the chicken under cold running water and pat dry with paper toweling. Sprinkle all over with salt and pepper and transfer to a plate.

In a bowl, combine 2 tablespoons of the oil, the mustard, honey, rosemary, and chile. Rub the mixture all over the chicken pieces, cover, and refrigerate for at least 3 hours or for up to overnight.

Remove the chicken from the refrigerator and bring to room temperature.

To make the Chardonnay Sauce, in a saucepan, combine the stock or broth and ½ cup of the wine. Bring to a boil over medium-high heat, then reduce the heat to medium-low and cook until the mixture is reduced to 1 cup, about 30 minutes. Stir in the peppercorns (if using).

In a small bowl, combine the remaining ½ cup wine with the cornstarch and whisk until smooth. Whisk the mixture into the stock mixture and cook, whisking constantly, until thickened to a sauce consistency, about 30 seconds. Season to taste with salt and ground pepper (if not using green peppercorns). Set aside.

Preheat an oven to 450 degrees F.

Heat a large, heavy ovenproof skillet over medium-high heat. When the pan is very hot, add the remaining 2 tablespoons oil. Add the chicken, skin side down, and cook until the skin is well browned, about 2 minutes. Turn the chicken, transfer the pan to the hot oven, and roast, without turning, just until the chicken is opaque throughout when cut into at the thickest part with a small, sharp knife and the skin is very crispy, 8 to 10 minutes.

Meanwhile reheat the Chardonnay Sauce over low heat.

Arrange the chicken on a warmed serving platter or individual plates, garnish with rosemary sprigs, and serve immediately. Pass the sauce at the table.

the CIA in the vines

The fact that Napa Valley is not merely America's premier wine region, but also a major culinary center, was confirmed by the decision of The Culinary Institute of America (CIA), based in Hyde Park, New York, to open a West Coast campus there in 1995.

The CIA has long been the country's leading teaching and training college for aspiring chefs. Its Napa Valley operation, devoted to the continuing education and career development of food and wine professionals, is located on Highway 29, just north of St. Helena, in Greystone Cellars, a massive, three-story stone building constructed in 1889. From 1950 to 1989, Greystone, which carries National Historical Landmark status, was owned by the Christian Brothers, who made sparkling wine there.

The CIA at Greystone facility harbors state-of-the-art teaching kitchens, a public restaurant, a demonstration auditorium, a retail store, and a museum. An extensive organic vegetable garden, sponsored by Sutter Home, a major benefactor of the CIA, provides student access to seasonal fresh produce. Organic fruits, herbs, and edible flowers are also grown on the property.

At the campus, professional chefs sharpen their skills in all facets of the culinary arts, from bread making and sauce preparation to cake decoration and wine service. There are classes on catering, institutional foodservice and management, and food photography and writing, as well as custom-designed courses for corporations, trade associations, and governmental agencies.

Naturally, proximity to many of America's finest wineries, which regularly host educational tastings for the students, fosters an understanding and appreciation of how fine wine complements and enhances fine cuisine.

hunter's chicken fricassee

SUGGESTED WINE: MERLOT OR ZINFANDEL | MAKES **4** SERVINGS

*Evalyn Trinchero suggests that her version of chicken cacciatore, an Italian classic that translates
as "hunter's style," can be made up to a day ahead. Cool the finished dish thoroughly, then cover
and refrigerate; reheat for 20 to 30 minutes over low heat.*

*While Evalyn uses a cut-up whole chicken for this dish, I prefer only thighs because they are not as
easily overcooked, as is common with breasts in stews. Most older versions of this dish leave the skin
intact, which adds great flavor but more fat. And for a thicker sauce, you can lightly dredge the
chicken pieces, with or without skin, in flour before browning. Serve the stew over pasta or polenta.*

INGREDIENTS

1 chicken (about 4 pounds), cut into serving pieces and skinned,
     or 8 skinned chicken thighs (see recipe introduction)

Salt

Freshly ground black pepper

1/4 cup olive oil

2 cups chopped white or yellow onion

1 teaspoon minced garlic

2 cups peeled, seeded, and chopped ripe or canned tomato with juices

4 ounces flavorful fresh mushrooms, such as porcino or
     portobello, tough stems discarded, thinly sliced

1/2 cup Merlot or Zinfandel

1 tablespoon chopped fresh flat-leaf parsley

1 tablespoon minced fresh rosemary, or 1 teaspoon
     crumbled dried rosemary

1 1/2 teaspoons minced fresh oregano, or 1/2 teaspoon
     crumbled dried oregano

Minced fresh flat-leaf parsley for garnish

Rinse the chicken under cold running water and pat dry with
paper toweling. Lightly sprinkle all over with salt and pepper.

Select a large skillet or other pan that will later hold all of
the chicken pieces without crowding them. Pour the oil into
the skillet and heat over medium-high heat until the oil is
almost smoking. Add the chicken and cook on one side until
well browned, about 2 minutes, then turn and brown the other
side, about 2 minutes longer. Using tongs, remove the chicken
to a plate and set aside.

Add the onion and garlic to the skillet and cook, stirring
frequently, until soft and golden, about 5 minutes. Stir in the
tomato and the reserved chicken and bring to a simmer, then
reduce the heat to maintain a simmer, cover tightly, and cook
for 30 minutes, stirring occasionally.

Stir the mushrooms, wine, chopped parsley, rosemary, oregano,
salt and pepper to taste into the chicken. Continue simmering,
partially covered, until the chicken is very tender when pierced
with a fork, about 20 minutes longer.

Remove the chicken pieces to a platter. If the sauce in the
pan is thin, increase the heat to medium-high and cook until
the mixture is somewhat thickened. Spoon the sauce over the
chicken and sprinkle with minced parsley.

duck and pork cassoulet

SUGGESTED WINE: PINOT NOIR OR MERLOT | MAKES **8** SERVINGS

My friend John Nyquist, one of Napa Valley's premier hosts, suggested the idea of a "pickup" version of cassoulet, the celebrated peasant dish from southwestern France, that relies on a few precooked components to help reduce the usual long preparation. Duck or goose confit can be prepared from a favorite recipe, ordered from a French restaurant or specialty meat market, or purchased canned imported from France in gourmet markets or through catalogs. Canned beans make an acceptable substitute for long-simmered ones.

INGREDIENTS

1$^{1}/_{2}$ pounds confit of duck or goose *(see recipe introduction)*

1 pound boneless pork tenderloin, trimmed of excess fat

2 tablespoons olive oil, or more if needed

1 pound high-quality duck, lamb, or pork sausage,
     sliced about 1 inch thick

1$^{1}/_{2}$ cups chopped white or yellow onion

$^{1}/_{2}$ cup chopped carrot

1 tablespoon minced garlic

$^{3}/_{4}$ cup Chardonnay

About 4 cups homemade chicken stock or canned
     reduced-sodium chicken broth

$^{3}/_{4}$ cup fresh or canned tomato puree

2 tablespoons tomato paste

1$^{1}/_{2}$ teaspoons minced fresh thyme, or $^{1}/_{2}$ teaspoon crumbled
     dried thyme

2 bay leaves

Cooking spray for greasing

8 cups cooked dried or canned small white beans such as
     flageolet or navy

Salt

Freshly ground black pepper

2 cups fine dried bread crumbs

$^{1}/_{2}$ cup minced fresh flat-leaf parsley

3 tablespoons unsalted butter or fat from the duck confit

Skin the duck or goose. Pull the meat off the bones and cut it into large bite-sized pieces. Set aside. Reserve the fat from the confit for later use.

Quickly rinse the pork under cold running water and pat dry with paper toweling. Cut into slices about ¾ inch thick and set aside.

In a sauté pan or heavy skillet, heat 2 tablespoons oil over medium-high heat. Add as many of the pork pieces as will fit in the pan without crowding and brown the meat on both sides, about 2 minutes per side. Transfer to a plate and set aside. Repeat with the remaining pork, then the sausage slices; add a little more oil as needed.

If necessary, add enough oil to the drippings in the same pan to equal 1 tablespoon. Add the onion and carrot and cook, stirring frequently, until the vegetables are soft but not browned, about 5 minutes. Add the garlic and cook for about 1 minute longer. Stir in the wine, reduce the heat to medium-low, and cook until the wine evaporates, about 5 minutes. Add 2 cups of the stock or broth, the tomato puree, tomato paste, thyme, and bay leaves. Increase the heat to medium-high and bring the mixture to a boil, then reduce the heat to achieve a simmer and simmer, uncovered, for about 5 minutes.

Preheat an oven to 325 degrees F. Generously coat a 13-inch round shallow earthenware casserole or a 13-by-9-inch baking dish with cooking spray and set aside.

Drain the beans in a colander set in a sink. If using canned beans, rinse under cold running water and drain again. Transfer the beans to a large bowl. Stir in the onion mixture and salt and pepper to taste.

Pour about half of the bean mixture into the prepared casserole or dish. Scatter the duck meat and browned pork and sausage over the beans. Top with the remaining bean mixture. Add enough of the remaining stock or broth to reach almost to the top of the beans.

In a bowl, combine the bread crumbs and parsley. Sprinkle about half of the mixture over the top of the beans; set the remaining mixture aside.

Transfer the casserole to the oven and bake for about 45 minutes.

Remove the casserole from the oven. Stir the casserole to incorporate the crumb topping into the other ingredients and smooth the top. Scatter the remaining crumb-parsley mixture over the top. Dot with the confit fat or butter. Return the casserole to the oven and bake until the top is brown and crusty and the juices are bubbly, 45 minutes to 1 hour. Add a little more stock or broth if needed during cooking to keep the beans from drying out.

Remove from the oven and let stand for about 10 minutes before serving.

chardonnay and cabernet

Napa Valley is renowned primarily for two wines: Cabernet Sauvignon and Chardonnay. Cabernet is the primary component of France's great red Bordeaux wines, while Chardonnay is the grape of its sublime white Burgundies. Both varieties are prominent in virtually every major wine-growing region of the world.

Of Napa's 36,000 vineyard acres, 20,000 are planted to Chardonnay and Cabernet. Over the past twenty years, a growing percentage of the valley's acreage has been planted or grafted to these two varieties, a reflection of their perfectibility in Napa's various soils and climates and of consumer demand.

Napa Valley Chardonnay and Cabernet vary depending upon where in the valley they are grown. In general, the best Chardonnays come from the cooler southern stretches, from the Carneros district to Oakville. Wines produced there boast bright citrus and apple aromas and flavors and better acidity than those from the warmer northern valley, which tend toward higher alcohol and riper, heavier flavors.

Conversely, the richest, most complex Cabernets usually issue from the north—Oakville to Calistoga—where warmer temperatures foster fully ripe grapes and the wines display layered cherry, currant, and dark chocolate aromas and flavors. Some of Napa's best Cabernets also come from hillside vineyards, which benefit from well-drained soils and low yields of small-berried clusters, resulting in perfumed, intensely flavored, long-lived red wines.

The best Napa Valley Chardonnays and Cabernets normally age for extended periods in small, often new, French and American oak barrels. This regimen imparts secondary textural and flavor elements (wood, tannin, and aromas of toast, vanilla, and spice) that mature and enrich the wines and create a more complex profile. Additionally, Napa Chardonnays often undergo a secondary "malolactic" fermentation, which converts appley malic acid to creamy lactic acid, yielding the smooth, buttery tone typical of the finest French Chardonnays.

Given the quality, popularity, and prevalence of both Chardonnay and Cabernet on restaurant wine lists, it's worth noting that they have limitations as accompaniments to food. For example, while Chardonnay pairs well with heavier fish, such as salmon or swordfish, and richly sauced chicken dishes, its flavors can overwhelm lighter entrées and are ill suited to spicy dishes. Conversely, the low acidity common to big, buttery Chardonnays may conspire with richly flavored foods to create a palate-dulling impression.

The flavors of Cabernet Sauvignon, although a fine match for simply prepared beef and game dishes, get muddled when confronted with spicy sauces or marinades, and the wine's sometimes-astringent tannins (the mouth-puckering sensation in red wines) can overwhelm lighter foods.

You may find Chardonnay and Cabernet exquisite accompaniments to your favorite dishes, but don't miss trying other delicious wine-food combinations. Some of Napa's other fine wines and the foods they best showcase are described on page 93.

pork tenderloin with pinot noir and prunes

SUGGESTED WINE: PINOT NOIR | MAKES **6** SERVINGS

The old and new Napa Valley are represented in this dish by prunes, a popular crop during Prohibition, and Pinot Noir, one of my favorite varietals from today's vineyards.

INGREDIENTS

2 pork tenderloins (about 1 pound each), trimmed of excess fat

Salt

Freshly ground black pepper

All-purpose flour for dredging

2 tablespoons olive oil

1 cup Pinot Noir

1 cup homemade chicken stock or canned reduced-sodium chicken broth

2 tablespoons honey

1 tablespoon Dijon mustard

1 cup bite-sized dried pitted prunes

2 tablespoons cold unsalted butter

Preheat an oven to 500 degrees F.

Quickly rinse the pork under cold running water and pat dry with paper toweling. Sprinkle lightly all over with salt and pepper and dredge lightly with flour.

In an ovenproof skillet, heat the oil over medium-high heat. Add the pork and cook, turning as needed, until browned on all sides, 5 to 8 minutes. Transfer the pan to the oven and roast for 5 minutes, then turn the meat and continue roasting until an instant-read thermometer inserted into the center of the tenderloins registers 135 degrees F, about 5 minutes longer.

Remove the skillet to a work surface. Transfer the tenderloins to a plate, cover with aluminum foil to keep warm, and set aside. Discard as much fat as possible from the skillet.

Place the skillet over medium-high heat. Stir in the wine, stock or broth, honey, and mustard and scrape up any browned bits from the bottom of the pan. Add the prunes and cook, stirring frequently, until the liquid is reduced by half, about 5 minutes.

Meanwhile, cut the tenderloins crosswise into slices about ¼ inch thick and arrange on warmed plates.

Remove the skillet from the heat, add the butter, and whisk until smooth. Taste the sauce and add salt and pepper if needed. Pour over the pork slices and serve immediately.

grilled leg of lamb with zinfandel marinade and mint pesto

SUGGESTED WINE: ZINFANDEL | MAKES **8** SERVINGS

Chef Jeffrey Starr urges the use of a sharp knife for chopping the mint to avoid bruising it and ruining the texture of the pesto. If the blade of your food processor is still very sharp, chop the mint in the machine.

INGREDIENTS

1 boned and butterflied leg of lamb (4 to 5 pounds)

5 garlic cloves, sliced into thin slivers

ZINFANDEL MARINADE

$1^1/_4$ cups Zinfandel

$^1/_2$ cup firmly packed light brown sugar

$^1/_3$ cup Dijon mustard

$^1/_4$ cup soy sauce

2 tablespoons chopped shallot

1 tablespoon minced fresh rosemary, or 1 teaspoon crumbled
    dried rosemary

1 tablespoon freshly ground black pepper

1 cup olive oil

Vegetable oil for brushing grill rack

MINT PESTO

1 cup finely chopped fresh mint

$^1/_4$ cup finely chopped unsalted dry-roasted peanuts

$^1/_4$ cup Asian sesame oil

2 tablespoons soy sauce

1 tablespoon unseasoned rice vinegar

1 tablespoon sugar

$1^1/_2$ teaspoons finely minced garlic

Salt

Freshly ground black pepper

recipe continues >>

>>

Quickly rinse the lamb under cold running water and pat dry with paper toweling. Trim off any excess fat. With a small, sharp knife, make ½-inch-deep slits every 2 inches around the entire surface of the meat and insert a garlic sliver in each slit. Transfer to a nonreactive (glass, stainless steel, or ceramic) container.

To make the Zinfandel Marinade, in a bowl, combine the wine, sugar, mustard, soy sauce, shallot, rosemary, and black pepper. Whisk in the olive oil. Pour the mixture over the lamb. Cover and refrigerate for 48 hours, turning the meat at least 3 times.

About 2 hours before grilling, remove the lamb from the refrigerator.

Prepare a covered grill for moderate indirect-heat cooking. Position a drip pan in the center of the fuel grate.

Remove the lamb from the marinade and set aside. Pour the marinade into a saucepan, place over medium-high heat, and bring to a boil, then set alongside the grill.

When the fire is ready, lightly brush the grill rack with vegetable oil. Place the lamb in the center of the rack, cover the grill, and cook, turning and brushing with the marinade every 10 minutes, until done to preference when cut into with a small, sharp knife, 35 to 40 minutes for medium-rare.

Meanwhile, to make the Mint Pesto, in a medium bowl, combine all of the pesto ingredients, including salt and pepper to taste. Transfer to a serving bowl and set aside.

Remove the lamb to a cutting surface, cover loosely with aluminum foil, and let stand for about 10 minutes.

To serve, thinly slice the lamb on the diagonal across the grain. Arrange the slices on a warmed serving platter and place the Mint Pesto alongside.

a range of whites and reds

Although Chardonnay, Cabernet Sauvignon, and, more recently, Merlot have come to dominate Napa Valley's vinous landscape, numerous other locally cultivated varieties provide a spectrum of choices for sublime wine-and-food pairings.

Fine renditions of Sauvignon Blanc, a lighter-bodied, crisper, less oaky wine than Chardonnay, typically offer bright, fresh citrus and melon flavors, often with a pungent, zesty sweet pepper or cut-grass aroma. Sauvignon Blanc is a good match for Caesar salad, raw oysters, grilled shrimp, lighter fish (trout, sole, snapper), simply prepared chicken and turkey dishes, and pasta with pesto.

A few Napa wineries make good dry-style Rieslings, which boast fragrant, blossomy (apple, honeysuckle) aromas and fruity, crisp flavors ideal for simple poultry, ham, and pork dishes, and for offsetting the spicy flavors of Asian cuisines. (Fruity wines with lower alcohol are usually better choices with spicy dishes than bone-dry wines of higher alcohol, which tend to ignite rather than tame the heat.)

Other wineries produce Gewürztraminer, a similarly fragrant, floral-smelling (rose petal, peach, and lichee) wine with fuller, spicier flavors than Riesling. If you had to choose one wine to accompany Indian or Thai food, Gewürztraminer would probably be the best bet.

The best "alternative" reds produced in Napa Valley are Pinot Noir, Zinfandel, Merlot, and Petite Syrah. Pinot Noir is a cool-climate variety that does best in the southern part of the valley, particularly the Carneros district that straddles both southwestern Napa and southeastern Sonoma counties and benefits from the cooling breezes of San Pablo Bay. Good Pinot Noir has an ethereal aroma of strawberries and raspberries, often with a delicate, tealike scent. The texture of the wine is supple and velvety, and the flavors suggest finesse and purity compared to the power and brawn of Napa Cabernets. Pinot Noir pairs well with an array of foods, including grilled salmon, herb-roasted chicken, baked ham, duck, and lamb.

A number of Napa wineries produce rich, spicy, berryish Zinfandels (the original red version), often from old hillside vines that yield small crops of intensely flavored grapes. These are big (often over 14 percent alcohol), bold wines that provide the perfect foil for robust fare, such as grilled red meats, burgers, hearty tomato-sauced pastas, pizzas, and strong cheeses.

In acreage and sales, Merlot has been the fastest-growing varietal in California over the past decade. Used by the French primarily as a blending grape, it offers aromas of cherry, mint, tea leaf, and tobacco that are similar to Cabernet, but with softer, rounder, earlier-maturing flavors. Merlot generally complements the same foods as Cabernet.

Finally, Petite Syrah, unrelated to the Syrah variety of France's Rhône Valley, produces an inky, rich, and robust red wine that partners well with red meats and other hearty fare.

wine-braised lamb shanks with figs

SUGGESTED WINE: MERLOT OR ZINFANDEL | MAKES **8** SERVINGS

*One of my favorite dishes for cold winter days in the valley, or elsewhere, is this complex-
flavored, meltingly tender lamb. Serve the meat over couscous, pasta, polenta, or rice and
sprinkle the slowly cooked shanks with gremolada to add fresh sparkle.*

INGREDIENTS

4 lamb shanks (about 1 pound each)

2 tablespoons olive oil

1 cup finely chopped red onion

1 teaspoon minced garlic

4 teaspoons all-purpose flour

1 tablespoon light brown sugar

1 teaspoon salt

1 teaspoon freshly ground black pepper

$1^1/2$ teaspoons minced fresh marjoram, or $^1/2$ teaspoon
    crumbled dried marjoram

$1^1/2$ teaspoons minced fresh rosemary, or $^1/2$ teaspoon
    crumbled dried rosemary

$1^1/2$ teaspoons minced fresh sage, or $^1/2$ teaspoon
    crumbled dried sage

$1^1/2$ teaspoons minced fresh thyme, or $^1/2$ teaspoon
    crumbled dried thyme

$^1/2$ teaspoon ground coriander

$^1/2$ teaspoon ground ginger

$^1/4$ teaspoon ground allspice

$^1/4$ teaspoon ground cloves

$^1/8$ teaspoon ground turmeric

1 cup Merlot or Zinfandel

$^1/2$ cup pureed fresh or canned tomato

1 teaspoon Worcestershire sauce

12 dried black Mission figs

GREMOLADA

3 tablespoons minced fresh flat-leaf parsley

1 tablespoon grated or minced fresh lemon zest

1 teaspoon minced garlic

Cut off as much fat and silvery skin as possible from the lamb shanks. Quickly rinse the shanks under cold running water, pat dry with paper toweling, and set aside.

In a heavy stew pot, heat the oil over medium-high heat. Add the onion and cook, stirring frequently, until soft and golden, about 8 minutes. Add the garlic and cook for about 1 minute longer. Remove from the heat and arrange the lamb shanks on top.

In a bowl, combine the flour, brown sugar, salt, pepper, marjoram, rosemary, sage, thyme, coriander, ginger, allspice, cloves, and turmeric and mix well. Add the wine, tomato puree, and Worcestershire sauce and blend well. Pour the mixture over the shanks. Place over medium-high heat and bring to a boil, then reduce the heat to achieve a simmer, cover tightly, and simmer for 1 hour.

Stir the figs into the pot and continue simmering until the meat is very tender and falling off the bones, about 1½ hours longer.

Remove the shanks to a work surface. Using metal tongs, pull the meat off the bones and return the meat to the pot; discard the bones.

Shortly before serving, prepare the Gremolada. In a small bowl, combine all of the ingredients and mix well.

To serve, ladle the stew into warmed bowls and sprinkle each serving with the Gremolada.

In 1948, when the Trinchero family began rejuvenating Sutter Home Winery, Napa Valley was entirely rural, with far more acres of prunes, walnuts, and tomatoes than grapes. Cattle roamed the valley floor. There were only a handful of wineries and tourism was nonexistent. In fact, Sutter Home became the first winery to offer tasting and sales of its products on the winery premises, a practice then viewed disapprovingly by other vintners in the valley.

"As a boy, I made extra money picking walnuts and prunes," recalls Bob Trinchero's brother, Roger, now Sutter Home's president. "Bob was in high school at the time, and he worked at the prune dehydrator south of town, as well as at the winery. The lifestyle then was a lot slower, and no one felt they were doing anything special. It's hard to imagine today, with five million people a year visiting the valley and packing our tasting rooms, but, until the 1970s, Napa Valley was definitely off the beaten path."

zinfandel beef and sausage stew *with polenta*

SUGGESTED WINE: ZINFANDEL | MAKES **6** SERVINGS

When flavorful fresh mushrooms are not available, Eralyn Trinchero suggests using dried porcini in this stew. To reconstitute, soak $^1/_2$ ounce dried mushrooms in $^1/_2$ cup lukewarm water for 15 minutes, then drain the mushrooms. Reserve the soaking liquid and use it as part of the hot water called for in the directions.

The oven method of making polenta is quicker and easier than the traditional stove-top stirring process.

INGREDIENTS

$1^1/_2$ pounds round or other boneless lean beef

$^3/_4$ pound sweet fennel Italian sausages

3 tablespoons olive oil

$^1/_4$ cup ($^1/_2$ stick) unsalted butter

2 ounces salt pork, cut into small dice, or sliced bacon, cut into small pieces

$1^1/_2$ cups finely chopped white or yellow onion

2 teaspoons minced garlic

$^1/_2$ cup chopped fresh flat-leaf parsley

$^1/_4$ teaspoon freshly ground black pepper

1 fresh or dried bay leaf, torn or crumbled

$1^1/_2$ cups Zinfandel

2 tablespoons minced celery

2 tablespoons minced carrot

$^1/_2$ cup peeled, seeded, drained, and finely chopped ripe or canned tomato

8 ounces flavorful fresh mushrooms such as porcino or portobello, tough stems discarded, sliced

2 quarts homemade chicken stock or canned reduced-sodium chicken broth (optional)

Salt

2 cups polenta

Pinch of freshly grated nutmeg

Minced fresh flat-leaf parsley for garnish

Quickly rinse the beef under cold running water and pat dry with paper toweling. Cut the beef into ½-inch cubes and set aside. Discard the casings from the sausages, cut into 1-inch-thick slices, and set aside.

In a large, heavy saucepan or stew pot, combine the oil, butter, and salt pork or bacon and place over medium-high heat. When the butter is melted, add the onion and cook, stirring frequently, until the onion is soft and golden, 8 to 10 minutes.

Add the beef cubes and sausage slices to the onion and cook, stirring frequently, until the meat is well browned, about 10 minutes. Add the garlic, chopped parsley, pepper, and bay leaf and cook for about 2 minutes longer. Stir in the wine, adjust the heat to achieve a simmer, cover, and simmer for 10 minutes.

Stir the celery, carrot, tomato, mushrooms, and 1½ cups hot water into the stew and continue simmering, covered, until the beef is tender, about 50 minutes. Add a little more hot water if necessary during cooking to keep the stew from drying out.

While the stew is simmering, prepare the polenta. Preheat an oven to 325 degrees F. In a large ovenproof pot or flame-proof casserole, combine the stock or broth (if using) or 2 quarts water with salt to taste and bring to a boil over high heat. Stir the liquid in one direction to create a whirlpool in the center. While stirring, slowly pour the polenta in a thin stream into the center of the swirling liquid until completely mixed. Return the mixture to a boil, cover tightly with a lid or aluminum foil, transfer to the oven, and bake until the polenta is thick and smooth, about 20 minutes. Remove from the oven and keep warm.

Uncover the stew, add the nutmeg, and simmer for about 10 minutes longer. Adjust the salt and pepper to taste.

To serve, scoop the polenta into warmed shallow bowls or onto warmed plates. Spoon the stew over the polenta and sprinkle each portion with minced parsley.

porcino-and-chile-crusted beef tri-tip
with caramelized onions

SUGGESTED WINE: CABERNET SAUVIGNON | MAKES **6** SERVINGS

Jeffrey Starr was one of the founding chefs at Mark Miller's Coyote Cafe in Santa Fe. That background comes through here in his recipe for a highly flavorful blend of dried porcini, smoky chipotle chile, and other seasonings rubbed onto the surface of the beef before roasting.

Chef Starr serves the sliced beef as a summer meal in the Sutter Home garden with three farmers' market salads—Mixed Greens with Verjus Vinaigrette (page 47), Heirloom Tomatoes with Basil, Feta, Olives, and Pine Nuts (page 52), and Roasted New Potato Salad (page 116).

INGREDIENTS

PORCINO-CHIPOTLE RUB

1 tablespoon freshly cracked black pepper

1 tablespoon crushed dried hot chile

1^1/$_2$ teaspoons ground cumin

1^1/$_2$ teaspoons crumbled dried thyme

1^1/$_2$ teaspoons dried onion flakes

1 teaspoon dried orange zest

^{1}/$_2$ teaspoon salt, or to taste

^{1}/$_4$ teaspoon freshly ground black pepper, or to taste

2 dried chipotle chiles, stems and seeds discarded

1 ounce dried porcino mushrooms

1 dried bay leaf

1 beef tri-tip roast (about 3 pounds)

Olive oil for brushing

CARAMELIZED ONIONS

3 tablespoons olive oil

4 pounds yellow onions, thinly sliced

^{1}/$_2$ cup Cabernet Sauvignon

2 tablespoons minced fresh thyme, or 2 teaspoons
    crumbled dried thyme

Salt

Freshly ground black pepper

To make the Porcino-Chipotle Rub, in a spice mill, combine all of the ingredients and grind to a coarse powder.

Quickly rinse the roast under cold running water and pat dry with paper toweling. Brush the roast all over with oil, then coat with the rub mixture and knead it into the meat. Cover loosely and refrigerate overnight.

About 1 hour before cooking, remove the roast from the refrigerator and set aside to come to room temperature.

To make the Caramelized Onions, in a heavy sauté pan or skillet, heat the oil over medium-low heat. Add the onions and cook, stirring occasionally, until deeply golden and caramelized, about 1 hour. Timing will vary according to the dryness of the onions. Add the wine and thyme and continue to cook until the wine is completely absorbed, about 10 minutes longer. Season to taste with salt and pepper. Set aside and reheat just before serving.

Position racks so that the roast will cook in the middle of an oven and preheat the oven to 350 degrees F.

Place the roast in a roasting pan, transfer to the oven, and roast until an instant-read thermometer inserted into the thickest part of the meat registers 135 degrees F (medium-rare), about 45 minutes.

Transfer the roast to a carving board, cover loosely with aluminum foil, and let stand for about 15 minutes.

Cut the roast against the grain into slices about ½ inch thick and drizzle with any collected meat juices. Reheat the onions and serve alongside.

prosciutto-wrapped tenderloin of beef cabernet

SUGGESTED WINE: CABERNET SAUVIGNON | MAKES **6** SERVINGS

Chef Jeffrey Starr created this succulent Cabernet Sauvignon–infused roast as the star of a Christmas dinner at the winery and teams it with Mashed Yukon Gold Potatoes and Celery Root (page 107) and Balsamic-Glazed Vegetables (page 114).

INGREDIENTS

1 beef tenderloin roast (about 3 pounds)

4 ounces prosciutto, very thinly sliced

2 tablespoons olive oil

2 tablespoons unsalted butter

1 cup finely chopped yellow onion

1 cup finely chopped celery

$1/2$ cup finely chopped carrot

1 tablespoon minced fresh thyme, or 1 teaspoon
   crumbled dried thyme

2 tablespoons minced garlic

2 cups Cabernet Sauvignon

1 cup rich homemade beef stock or canned beef broth

Salt

Freshly ground black pepper

Quickly rinse the beef under cold running water and pat dry with paper toweling. Trim off any excess fat. Wrap the beef with the prosciutto, overlapping the pieces until the roast is covered from end to end. Tie cotton string around the circumference of the roast in several places to secure the prosciutto.

In a 3-quart saucepan or a stew pot just large enough to hold the roast, combine the oil and butter. Place over medium heat until the butter begins to foam. Add the roast and brown well on all sides. Remove the roast to a plate.

Add the onion, celery, carrot, thyme, and garlic to the same pan and cook, stirring frequently, until the vegetables are soft and golden, about 8 minutes. Return the roast to the pan and add the wine, stock or broth, and salt and pepper to taste. Increase the heat to medium-high and bring to a simmer, then adjust the heat to maintain a very gentle simmer, cover, and simmer for 12 minutes. Turn the roast and continue simmering until an instant-read thermometer inserted into the center of the roast registers 135 degrees F (medium-rare), about 12 minutes longer.

Using metal tongs, transfer the roast to a carving board, cover loosely with aluminum foil, and let rest for about 15 minutes.

Meanwhile, increase the heat to medium-high and cook the braising liquid, stirring frequently, for about 10 minutes. Pour through a fine-mesh strainer into a clean saucepan, pressing against the solids with a spoon to release as much juice as possible. Return to the heat and cook, stirring occasionally, until reduced to a velvety light sauce, about 5 minutes longer. Season to taste with salt and pepper. Keep warm.

Remove the strings from the roast and slice crosswise into 6 equal pieces. Arrange the beef on a warmed platter or individual plates and spoon the sauce over the top.

portobello burger

SUGGESTED WINE: CABERNET SAUVIGNON OR ZINFANDEL | MAKES **4** SERVINGS

In 1994, Kurt Wait, from Redwood City, California, impressed my fellow cook-off judges (food critic Michael Bauer, cookbook author Marion Cunningham, and chefs Mark Miller of Santa Fe's Coyote Cafe and Judy Rodgers of San Francisco's Zuni Cafe) and me enough with this recipe to capture the $10,000 Grand Prize of Sutter Home's Build a Better Burger competition. A couple of years later, we all watched with pride as Kurt went on to win the first $1,000,000 prize in the Pillsbury Bake-Off.

INGREDIENTS

SUN-DRIED TOMATO MAYONNAISE

1/3 cup mayonnaise

1/4 cup chopped drained sun-dried tomatoes packed in olive oil

MUSHROOMS

2 tablespoons chopped fresh thyme, or 2 teaspoons
     crumbled dried thyme

1 tablespoon chopped fresh oregano, or 1 teaspoon
     crumbled dried oregano

1 teaspoon salt

1 teaspoon freshly ground black pepper

1/4 cup Zinfandel

2 tablespoons olive oil

1 teaspoon grated or minced fresh lemon zest

4 large fresh portobello mushrooms, stemmed

1 1/2 pounds ground chuck

3 tablespoons Zinfandel

2 shallots, finely chopped

2 teaspoons ground cumin

1/4 teaspoon ground cayenne

4 round focaccia rolls or onion rolls, split

Vegetable oil for brushing grill rack

16 arugula leaves

4 ounces creamy mild goat cheese

Prepare an open grill for moderate direct-heat cooking.

To make the Sun-Dried Tomato Mayonnaise, in a small bowl, combine the mayonnaise and tomatoes; set aside.

To prepare the mushrooms, in a cup, stir together the thyme, oregano, salt, and pepper. In a medium bowl, whisk 1 tablespoon of the spice mixture with the wine, olive oil, and lemon zest; reserve the remaining spice mixture for use in the patties. Add the mushrooms and turn to coat with the marinade; set aside.

In a large bowl, combine the reserved spice mixture with the ground chuck, wine, shallots, cumin, and cayenne. Shape into 4 round patties to fit the rolls.

When the fire is ready, brush the grill rack with oil. Drain the mushrooms, reserving the marinade. Place the mushrooms and patties on the rack. Grill the mushrooms, brushing frequently with the marinade and turning once, until tender, 5 to 10 minutes. Grill the patties, brushing frequently with the marinade and turning once, until done to preference, 8 to 10 minutes for medium-rare. During the last few minutes of cooking, place the rolls, cut side down, on the outer edges of the grill until lightly toasted.

Spread the Sun-Dried Tomato Mayonnaise on the cut sides of the rolls. Top each roll bottom with 4 arugula leaves and a patty. Spread each patty with one-fourth of the cheese. Top each with a mushroom, then the roll top.

siciliano burger *with fresh ciliegine and sweet tomato butter*

SUGGESTED WINE: MERLOT OR ZINFANDEL | MAKES **6** SERVINGS

There was no cook-off held for the Build a Better Burger competition in 1997. Instead, after the ten best recipes were selected, I grilled and ranked each burger. In spite of some excellent competitors, this recipe from Susan Asanovic of Wilton, Connecticut, was the clear winner. In the press release on her victory, I stated that her Sweet Tomato Butter was so good it should be bottled for sale.

Ciliegine, small fresh balls of mozzarella packed in water, are available at cheese shops, Italian markets, and some supermarkets.

INGREDIENTS

SWEET TOMATO BUTTER

$3/4$ cup drained sun-dried tomatoes packed in olive oil,
   plus 2 tablespoons oil

1 teaspoon mild honey

$1/2$ cup green or red seedless grapes

About 2 tablespoons small capers, rinsed and drained (optional)

$1/2$ cup chopped fresh flat-leaf parsley

Salt

Freshly ground black pepper

1 pound ground veal

$3/4$ pound extra-lean ground beef

4 cloves garlic, crushed

$1/2$ cup fresh Italian bread crumbs (from about 1 ounce bread)

$1/4$ cup pine nuts

1 teaspoon ground cinnamon

Large pinch of ground cayenne

1 teaspoon dried rosemary, ground in spice grinder

1 teaspoon kosher salt, or to taste

Freshly ground black pepper

Six $1/3$-ounce unsalted fresh mozzarella balls *(ciliegine)*

Vegetable oil for brushing grill rack

12 radicchio leaves

Six 3-by-4-inch sections crusty Italian bread, preferably
   rosemary-semolina, sliced lengthwise in half

To make the Sweet Tomato Butter, in a food processor, combine the tomatoes and 2 tablespoons of their oil. Add the honey and grapes and process to a smooth paste. Mix in the capers (if using), parsley, and salt and pepper to taste. Transfer to a bowl and set aside.

Prepare an open grill for moderate direct-heat cooking.

In a large bowl, combine the veal, beef, garlic, bread crumbs, pine nuts, cinnamon, cayenne, rosemary, and salt and pepper to taste. Mix well. Divide the mixture into 6 equal portions and flatten each into a disk. Center 1 mozzarella ball in the center of each patty and enclose the cheese in the middle. Flatten to form patties ¾ inch thick. Set aside.

When the fire is ready, brush the grill rack with oil. Place the patties on the rack and grill, turning once, until done to preference, 8 to 10 minutes for medium-rare. Brush the radicchio lightly with some of the oil from the tomatoes and grill until charred but still crisp, about 4 minutes. Place the bread, cut side down, around the edges of the grill and toast.

Spread the cut sides of the bread generously with Sweet Tomato Butter. Top each bottom slice of bread with a patty and a radicchio leaf, then the top slice of bread.

In Napa Valley, as in all agricultural communities, everything culminates in the harvest. From early August, when the first grapes for sparkling wine are picked, to late October, when the last Cabernet Sauvignon clusters are plucked from russet-leaved vines, the valley is consumed with bringing in the grapes.

During the height of harvest, grape pickers outfitted with knives, buckets, and boxes move through the vineyards, first detaching the fat, glistening grapes and then conveying their treasure. Trucks laden with fruit clog the valley's two main thoroughfares, and winery workers labor overtime to turn juice to wine before the next load arrives.

Will the weather cooperate? Is it warm enough for all the fruit to ripen before fall rains arrive? Did heavy spring rain foster mold and rot in the clusters? Is the crop too small or too large? Is there enough tank space should all the varieties ripen at once? These are the questions that torment growers and vintners as they work virtually nonstop throughout the harvest months, subsisting on sandwiches, pizza, coffee, and the winemaker's favorite summer beverage, beer.

In the fall, after the fruit has been picked, a driver down Highway 29 or the Silverado Trail may believe that he or she is actually inside a winery, for a thousand percolating fermentations fill the air with a musky perfume that lasts for weeks. The fragrance only subsides as fall turns into winter, leaves drop from vines, and vintners retreat to rest, tend to their new wines, and replenish their resources for the next harvest, which will arrive before they know it.

mashed yukon gold potatoes and celery root

SUGGESTED WINE: CHARDONNAY OR PINOT NOIR | MAKES **6** SERVINGS

Jeffrey Starr's combination of buttery yellow potatoes and creamy celery root (celeriac) makes a rich and satisfying accompaniment to roasted chicken and meats.

INGREDIENTS

1 pound Yukon Gold potatoes, peeled and cut into 1-inch pieces

1 pound celery root, peeled and cut into 1-inch pieces

$^3/_4$ cup heavy (whipping) cream

6 tablespoons ($^3/_4$ stick) unsalted butter, melted

Salt

Freshly ground black pepper

In a large saucepan, combine the potatoes and celery root and add water to cover completely. Place over high heat and bring to a boil, then adjust the heat to maintain a simmer and cook until the vegetables are tender when pierced with a fork or wooden skewer, about 15 minutes.

Drain the potato-celery root mixture and return to the saucepan. Place over low heat and shake the pan to evaporate excess water, about 1 minute. Stir in the cream and cook, stirring and scraping the bottom of the pan occasionally to prevent scorching, for about 10 minutes.

Put the mixture through a potato ricer or food mill into a metal bowl. Add the butter and salt and pepper to taste. Using a wooden spoon or a hand mixer, whip the mixture until light and fluffy.

Transfer to a serving bowl and serve immediately. (Alternatively, cover the metal bowl with aluminum foil and place over a pan of simmering water to keep warm for up to 30 minutes, then transfer to a serving bowl.)

liquid sunshine

Wine is Napa Valley's most famous product, but the region is also becoming known for another prized liquid: olive oil.

During the late nineteenth century, thousands of olive trees graced the valley, and there was a significant trade in olive oil. Early in the twentieth century, however, the valley olive oil production was squelched by the far cheaper imports from Europe. After Prohibition, when Napa began its transformation into a wine-producing monoculture, olive trees, many on winery property, were either uprooted or abandoned.

In the early 1990s, a number of local olive oil aficionados, many of them vintners, began restoring the old olive trees, planting new groves, and studying olive harvesting and production techniques.

Today, there are approximately sixty olive growers and a dozen commercial producers, including Sutter Home, of quality olive oil in the valley. They are importing and planting Italian olive varieties (in addition to the Mission, Manzanillo, and Sevillano varieties common in California), visiting Italy and Spain to learn the trade, and joining together to promote their products.

The California Olive Oil Council, which promotes the state's oils, has established an expert tasting panel to assess the quality of California oils. The council also issues seals of approval for those meriting the extra-virgin designation. These oils, rendered from the first pressing of the fruit, contain less than 1 percent acidity and are free of defects. High-quality California oils, including those from the valley, can be purchased at gourmet food stores everywhere. Visitors to Napa Valley can find a good selection of oils at Oakville Grocery and Dean & DeLuca in St. Helena and at some winery tasting rooms.

Despite the renaissance of Napa Valley olive oil, it is unlikely olive trees will ever displace the valley's grapevines. A ton of olives, after pressing, yields just 30 gallons of oil, while a ton of grapes, which is more highly valued from the beginning, produces 150 to 170 gallons. Nonetheless, diners these days at Napa's many fine restaurants are likely to begin their meals with a glass of Napa Valley wine, a hunk of locally baked bread, and a saucer of fruity Napa Valley olive oil.

grilled asparagus *with sesame mayonnaise*

SUGGESTED WINE: CHENIN BLANC OR GEWÜRZTRAMINER | MAKES 8 SERVINGS

Tender asparagus stalks herald spring in the wine country. After grilling lamb or other meat, Jeffrey Starr cooks asparagus over the still-glowing coals.

A grill tray (see page 49) will keep the asparagus from falling through the grill rack into the fire. If you choose not to use a tray, position the asparagus spears perpendicular to the bars of the grill rack.

INGREDIENTS

SESAME MAYONNAISE

$2/3$ cup mayonnaise

2 tablespoons Asian sesame oil

1 tablespoon soy sauce

2 teaspoons freshly squeezed lemon juice

2 teaspoons minced green onion, including green tops

Freshly ground black pepper

2 tablespoons sesame seed

48 asparagus spears, tough ends discarded

3 tablespoons olive oil

Salt

Freshly ground black pepper

Vegetable oil for brushing grill tray

To make the Sesame Mayonnaise, in a bowl, combine all of the mayonnaise ingredients, including pepper to taste. Transfer to a small serving bowl, cover, and refrigerate for up to 2 days.

In a small skillet, place the sesame seed over medium heat and toast, shaking the pan or stirring frequently, until lightly golden and fragrant, about 5 minutes. Pour onto a plate to cool and set aside.

Prepare a covered grill for low direct-heat cooking.

In a bowl, toss the asparagus with the olive oil and season to taste with salt and pepper.

When the fire is ready, position a grill tray on the grill rack and brush it with vegetable oil. Place the asparagus on the tray and grill, turning once, until tender when pierced with a small, sharp knife, 5 to 10 minutes, depending upon size.

To serve, arrange the asparagus on a serving platter and sprinkle with the toasted sesame seed. Offer the Sesame Mayonnaise alongside.

garlicky stuffed artichokes

SUGGESTED WINE: SAUVIGNON BLANC | MAKES 8 SERVINGS

Big California artichokes redolent with a garlic-and-bread-crumb filling go well with nearly any hearty main dish. Evalyn Trinchero uses the same stuffing mixture to fill mushroom caps, then drizzles them with olive oil and broils them until tender.

INGREDIENTS

Juice of 1 lemon

4 large artichokes

2 teaspoons chopped garlic

1/2 cup chopped fresh flat-leaf parsley

2 cups fresh bread crumbs, preferably from French or Italian
    bread

1/4 cup freshly grated Parmesan cheese (about 1 ounce),
    preferably Parmigiano-Reggiano

6 tablespoons olive oil

Salt

In a large bowl, pour in enough cold water to cover all of the artichokes once they are added. Add the lemon juice and set aside.

Cut off and discard all but about 1/3 inch of the stem from each artichoke. Snap off the tough lower leaves. Then, using scissors, cut off the outer part of each remaining leaf, leaving only the pale greenish edible portion near the base. As you work toward the choke, the edible portion becomes longer. Cut each artichoke lengthwise in half and scrape away the thin inner leaves and fuzzy choke. As soon as each artichoke is prepared, drop it into the bowl of lemon water to prevent darkening.

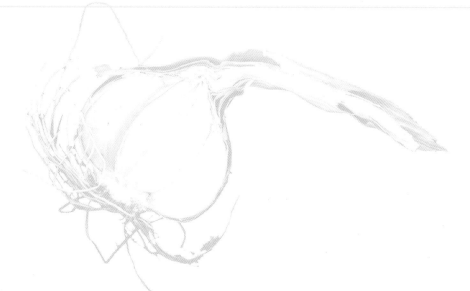

In a food processor, combine the garlic and parsley and process until finely chopped. Add the bread crumbs and cheese and blend well. With the motor running, slowly drizzle in ¼ cup of the olive oil, about 1 tablespoon at a time, until the mixture is moist enough to hold its shape.

Remove the artichokes from the lemon water and pat dry with paper toweling. Spoon the bread mixture into the artichoke cavities, then transfer the artichoke halves, stuffed side up, to a large skillet. Pour water into the skillet to a depth of 1 inch. Drizzle the artichokes with the remaining 2 tablespoons olive oil and sprinkle with salt to taste.

Cover the skillet with a tight-fitting lid, place over low heat, and cook until the artichokes are tender when pierced with a wooden skewer, about 45 minutes. Serve warm.

VARIATION

Remove the stems from about 16 cremini or other fresh mushrooms about 2 inches in diameter. Using a teaspoon, mound the bread stuffing in the mushroom cavities, pressing slightly to firm. Place the mushrooms, stuffed side up, on a nonstick baking sheet, drizzle with olive oil, and broil until the filling is lightly browned and the mushrooms are tender, 4 to 6 minutes. Serve warm.

summer squash gratin

SUGGESTED WINE: SAUVIGNON BLANC OR CHARDONNAY | MAKES **6** SERVINGS

*Feel free to substitute other good-melting cheeses such as Fontina or white Cheddar in this
old-fashioned dish that goes well with barbecued or grilled foods.*

INGREDIENTS

2$^1/_2$ pounds zucchini or other summer squash,
    sliced about $^1/_4$ inch thick

Salt

Cooking spray for greasing

2 tablespoons olive oil

1 cup finely chopped white or yellow onion

1 teaspoon minced garlic

1 cup Sauvignon Blanc or Chardonnay

1$^1/_2$ cups freshly shredded Gruyère cheese (about 4$^1/_2$ ounces)

1 tablespoon minced fresh marjoram or oregano, or 1 teaspoon
    crumbled dried marjoram or oregano

$^1/_2$ teaspoon freshly ground black pepper, or to taste

$^1/_2$ cup fine dried bread crumbs, preferably from French
    or Italian bread

1 tablespoon unsalted butter, cut into small pieces

Place the squash in a colander set over a bowl or in a sink,
sprinkle with salt, toss to distribute the salt, and let stand
for about 30 minutes to draw out excess moisture.

Preheat an oven to 350 degrees F. Lightly grease an 8-by-10-
inch or other 2-quart shallow baking dish with cooking
spray and set aside.

Gather the squash in your hands and squeeze gently to release
as much liquid as possible, then pat dry with paper toweling
and set aside.

In a skillet or sauté pan, heat the oil over medium-high heat.
Add the onion and cook, stirring frequently, until soft but
not browned, about 5 minutes. Add the squash, garlic, and
wine and cook, stirring frequently, until the liquid is evaporated and the squash is tender, about 10 minutes.

Stir the cheese, herb, and pepper into the squash mixture
and mix well. Transfer the mixture to the prepared dish and
distribute evenly. Sprinkle the bread crumbs evenly over the
top, then dot with the butter.

Bake until the cheese is bubbly and the crumb topping is
crisp, about 20 minutes.

white zinfandel serendipity

During the late 1960s, a competition of sorts emerged among California wineries to see who could produce the biggest, most intensive Zinfandels from Amador County's old vines. "We were all trying to 'out Zin' one another," Bob Trinchero recalls.

Bob's approach, in 1972, was to draw off some of the free-run juice produced right after crushing the grapes and prior to fermentation. Long employed by French vintners, this technique, called *saignée*, intensifies the color, body, and flavor of red wine by decreasing the amount of juice relative to the amount of skins.

The method worked beautifully, and the 1972 Sutter Home Zinfandel was a marvelously dark, rich wine. But it left Bob with 550 gallons of pale juice, which he fermented to dryness. Not quite knowing what to do with the wine, Bob bottled it and sold it in the winery tasting room as *Oeil de Perdrix*, French for "Eye of the Partridge." The novel wine did not meet with instant acceptance. Most who sampled it found it dry and austere. Not known for giving up easily, Bob made the wine again in 1974. Once again it generated a tepid response.

In 1975, however, what Bob Trinchero alternately calls "serendipity" or "a fortuitous accident" occurred. That year, the pale Zinfandel suffered a "stuck fermentation," a situation in which not all the grape sugar converted to alcohol. Despite his best efforts, Bob could not get the wine to complete the process, so he bottled it as it was, with about 2 percent residual sugar and a tinge of pink. This subtle change in taste and appearance transformed his customers' opinion of the wine. Suddenly, they were buying bottles of it, then coming back for cases.

By 1987, Sutter Home White Zinfandel had become the best-selling wine in the United States. The Trincheros' success spawned an army of emulative "blush" wines and, also serendipitously, preserved many old Zinfandel vineyards that otherwise would have been torn out. Today, those vineyards are producing magnificent red Zinfandels in addition to White Zinfandel, which is the second most popular wine in the nation, with annual sales of over 21 million cases.

When asked what makes White Zinfandel so popular, Bob Trinchero offers a simple explanation, "it tastes good." To a generation raised on soft drinks, the light, fresh, fruity, chillable beverage is an easily understood, user-friendly introduction to wine. Although derided by wine sophisticates, it clearly strikes a chord among novice wine drinkers. "White Zinfandel taught me an important lesson," says Bob, "which is that success in the wine business depends upon making wines that appeal to the tastes of your customers, rather than to your own." The almost half a billion bottles of Sutter Home White Zinfandel sold to date attest to the truth of Bob's philosophy.

balsamic-glazed vegetables

SUGGESTED WINE: CHENIN BLANC OR GEWÜRZTRAMINER | MAKES **6** TO **8** SERVINGS

In this preparation, chef Jeffrey Starr uses balsamic vinegar, a popular wine-country ingredient, along with soy sauce and brown sugar to add special flavor to roasted vegetables.

INGREDIENTS

5 pounds assorted vegetables such as beets, carrots, garlic,
    mushrooms, onions, parsnips, potatoes, shallots, and
    sweet peppers
Vegetable oil for greasing
2 tablespoons olive oil
1 tablespoon unsalted butter, melted
2 tablespoons soy sauce
2 tablespoons light brown sugar
1 tablespoon balsamic vinegar
Salt
Freshly ground black pepper
1/4 cup chopped fresh chives

To prepare the vegetables, peel beets, carrots, parsnips, or other root vegetables and cut into 1-inch pieces. Peel shallots or garlic cloves and leave whole. Cut peeled large onions into quarters, or leave peeled pearl onions whole. Stem mushrooms and leave whole or cut large ones into 1-inch pieces. Remove the stems, seeds, and membranes from sweet peppers and cut into 1-inch pieces.

Preheat an oven to 375 degrees F. Using a pastry brush, generously grease a rimmed baking sheet or shallow baking pan with vegetable oil.

In a large bowl, combine the olive oil, butter, soy sauce, brown sugar, and vinegar and mix well. Add the vegetables and toss to coat all over. Using a slotted spoon, transfer the vegetables to the prepared baking sheet or pan, arranging them in a single layer. Reserve the remaining oil mixture. Sprinkle with salt and pepper to taste.

Transfer to the oven and roast, stirring and basting occasionally with the reserved oil mixture, until the vegetables are tender when pierced with a wooden skewer or fork, about 1 hour.

To serve, transfer the vegetables to a warmed serving bowl, taste, and add more salt and pepper if needed. Add the chives, toss well, and serve.

roasted new potato salad *with champagne vinaigrette*

SUGGESTED WINE: SAUVIGNON BLANC | MAKES **6** SERVINGS

Champagne vinegar adds an elegant touch to the fruity olive oil dressing for this great summer side dish. Chef Jeffrey Starr often adds small, young green beans that have been blanched until crisp-tender.

INGREDIENTS

3 pounds small new potatoes, preferably assorted white,
    yellow, red, and purple varieties of similar size

3 tablespoons olive oil

Salt

Freshly ground black pepper

1 cup tiny cherry tomatoes such as Currant or Sweet 100

1 cup croutons

$1/2$ cup chopped green onion, including green tops

$1/4$ cup freshly grated Asiago cheese

CHAMPAGNE VINAIGRETTE

$1/4$ cup Champagne vinegar

2 tablespoons Dijon mustard

12 fresh basil leaves

3 garlic cloves

2 flat anchovy fillets packed in olive oil, rinsed and patted dry

$1/2$ cup extra-virgin olive oil

Salt

Freshly ground black pepper

Preheat an oven to 350 degrees F.

If the potatoes are not of uniform size, cut any larger ones to equal the smallest ones; they should all be large bite-sized pieces.

In a bowl, toss the potatoes with the oil, then add salt and pepper to taste. Place in a shallow roasting pan and roast, stirring occasionally, until tender when pierced with a wooden skewer or fork, about 30 minutes.

Transfer the pan to a work surface to cool completely.

Transfer the cooled potatoes to a bowl. Add the tomatoes, croutons, green onion, and cheese and toss well.

To make the Champagne Vinaigrette, in a blender or food processor, combine the vinegar, mustard, basil, garlic, and anchovy and blend until smooth. With the motor running, drizzle in the olive oil in a steady stream and process until incorporated. Season to taste with salt and pepper.

Pour the dressing over the potato mixture and toss to blend well. Taste and add more salt and pepper if needed.

Serve at room temperature.

white and wild rice salad *with ginger-citrus dressing*

SUGGESTED WINE: CHENIN BLANC OR GEWÜRZTRAMINER | MAKES 8 SERVINGS

An Asian-inspired dressing enlivens this blend of white rice and the aquatic grass seed known as wild rice. For Sutter Home parties, Jeffrey Starr allows the salad to stand for about 3 hours before serving to allow the flavors to blend.

INGREDIENTS

2 cups freshly cooked long-grain white rice, at room temperature

2 cups freshly cooked wild rice, at room temperature

$1/2$ cup chopped green onion, including green tops

$1/2$ cup halved seedless grapes

$1/4$ cup dried apricots, cut into narrow strips

$1/4$ cup chopped red sweet pepper

$1/4$ cup chopped roasted cashews

3 tablespoons chopped fresh cilantro *(coriander)*

GINGER-CITRUS DRESSING

$1/4$ cup freshly squeezed orange juice

2 tablespoons unseasoned rice vinegar

$1^1/2$ tablespoons soy sauce

1 tablespoon minced fresh ginger

1 tablespoon Dijon mustard

1 tablespoon light brown sugar

$1^1/2$ teaspoons minced garlic

$1/2$ cup Asian sesame oil

Salt

Freshly ground black pepper

In a large bowl, combine the white rice, wild rice, onion, grapes, apricots, sweet pepper, cashews, and cilantro and toss to mix thoroughly.

To make the Ginger-Citrus Dressing, in a bowl, combine the orange juice, vinegar, soy sauce, ginger, mustard, sugar, and garlic and whisk to blend thoroughly. Whisk in the oil and season to taste with salt and pepper.

Pour the dressing over the rice mixture and toss well. Cover and set aside for at least one hour or for up to 3 hours before serving.

sweets

This collection of desserts highlights the fruits of Napa Valley's home orchards: crisp apples, buttery pears, ripe figs, luscious peaches, Meyer lemons, and satiny persimmons.

Goat's milk, used to make creamy valley cheeses, is used here in a tangy version of flan, a caramel-glazed custard introduced by residents who came from Mexico. Lavender, which grows rampant in the Mediterranean, also blooms profusely in the similar environs of the valley. I've added the herb's seductive fragrance and flavor to gelato to create an exotic dessert.

Triple Cream, a spiced sherry made by Sutter Home, adds a unique flavor to tiramisu, one of Napa Valley's favorite sweets, and to zabaglione, a classic of the Piedmont. Moscato, another dessert wine, is used to infuse a mélange of summer fruits.

Two cookie recipes from the Trinchero family collection feature valley walnuts, still harvested from the remnants of commercial orchards from the Prohibition era, and almonds from nearby valleys. The cookies go great with several of the other desserts, or can star on their own with a glass of dessert wine.

moscato-infused fruits

MAKES **6** SERVINGS

The success of this simple presentation, one of my favorite summer desserts, depends upon the quality of the fruit. Choose perfectly ripe soft summer fruits such as figs, apricots, nectarines, peaches, or raspberries; be sure to peel the peaches. Cut the stone fruits into bite-sized pieces and the figs into halves or quarters. Add each fruit to the wine as soon as it is sliced to prevent darkening. Adjust the amount of sugar according to the sweetness of the fruits.

Serve one type of fruit or a colorful mixture in oversized goblets and offer Amaretti (page 134), biscotti, or other crisp cookies or pound cake for dipping into the fruity wine.

INGREDIENTS

1 bottle (750 ml) Moscato

$^1/_2$ cup sugar, or to taste

1 teaspoon finely grated or minced fresh lemon zest

8 cups sliced ripe summer fruits (see recipe introduction)

3 tablespoons torn fresh mint leaves

Fresh mint sprigs for garnish

In a large bowl, combine the wine, sugar, and lemon zest and stir to blend well. Add the fruits and stir gently to coat well. Cover tightly and refrigerate for up to 4 hours.

About 1 hour before serving, add the torn mint and gently toss the fruit.

To serve, divide the fruit and liquid evenly among 6 large goblets and garnish each serving with mint sprigs.

fresh fig and peach galettes

SUGGESTED WINE: MOSCATO OR LATE-HARVEST RIESLING | MAKES **6** SERVINGS

One of the things I miss most about living in Napa Valley is the bountiful harvest from several fig trees that grew in my garden. Here, my favorite late-summer fruit is teamed with perfectly ripe peaches in free-form tarts for eating out of hand. Alternatively, substitute all peaches or all figs for the combination, or use nectarines, raspberries, or other soft fruits for the filling.

If you prefer smaller galettes, divide the dough into 8 equal portions.

INGREDIENTS

SWEET TART PASTRY

3$\frac{1}{2}$ cups all-purpose flour

6 tablespoons sugar

$\frac{3}{4}$ teaspoon salt

1 tablespoon grated or minced fresh lemon zest

1$\frac{1}{2}$ cups (3 sticks) chilled unsalted butter, cut into small pieces

3 egg yolks, lightly beaten

About 6 tablespoons iced water

PEACH FILLING

2 pounds ripe peaches, peeled, pitted, and sliced

1 pound ripe figs, stemmed and cut lengthwise into
    halves or quarters

About 6 tablespoons sugar

2 tablespoons cornstarch, potato starch, or quick-cooking tapioca

2 teaspoons pure vanilla extract (optional)

Sugar for sprinkling

Position racks so that the tarts will bake in the middle of an oven and preheat the oven to 400 degrees F. Line 2 baking sheets with kitchen parchment and set aside.

To make the Sweet Tart Pastry, combine the flour, sugar, salt, lemon zest, and butter in a food processor. Pulse just until the mixture is well blended and resembles cornmeal. With the machine running, add the egg yolks through the feed tube, then add just enough of the iced water, about 1 tablespoon at a time, until the dough begins to gather into a shaggy mass.

Alternatively, combine the flour, sugar, salt, lemon zest, and butter in a bowl and, using a pastry blender or your fingertips, work the ingredients together until the mixture resembles cornmeal. Then, using a fork, blend in the egg yolks and enough iced water to form a shaggy mass that begins to hold together.

recipe continues >>

>>

Working quickly, form the dough into a ball, then divide it into 6 equal pieces. Using your fingertips, shape each piece of dough into a disk and cover with a cloth kitchen towel or plastic wrap to keep the dough from drying out.

Working with 1 piece at a time, roll the dough out on a lightly floured board into a round about ⅛ inch thick and about 7 inches in diameter. It is not necessary to trim any rough edges. Transfer to a prepared baking sheet. Repeat with the remaining dough pieces. Cover the baking sheets with a towel or plastic wrap to keep the dough from drying out.

In a bowl, combine the peaches, figs, sugar to taste, the cornstarch, potato starch, or tapioca, and the vanilla (if using) and mix gently. Spoon the mixture onto the center of each dough round, dividing equally and leaving a 2-inch border of dough all the way around the edges. Bring the edges of the pastry up and over the fruit as far as possible, leaving the fruit exposed in the center. Pinch the dough to form pleats that make the pastry fit snugly around the fruit. Sprinkle the exposed pastry generously with sugar.

Bake until the pastry is golden brown and the fruit is tender and bubbling, about 25 minutes.

Transfer to a wire rack to cool to room temperature.

dessert wines

Although Napa Valley is best known for its marvelous dry table wines, many wineries, including Sutter Home, also produce delightful dessert wines. My preference is to serve one of these nectars on its own after the dessert is finished or to pour it in place of a sweet. But these wines are more often poured as fine companions to the array of sinfully delectable desserts prepared by the valley's chefs, ranging from fresh-fruit compote and tiramisu to countless tarts, tortes, and cakes. Whatever the dessert, there is a Napa Valley Moscato, late- harvest Riesling, or port that will elevate it from the merely heavenly to the simply divine.

When pairing a dessert and a dessert wine, keep in mind that the wine should always be sweeter than the dessert. Otherwise, the wine will taste too dry and perhaps even harsh.

Quality dessert wines usually display captivatingly fragrant aromas, which can be obliterated or dulled by overchilling. And because dessert wines are often extremely sweet and rich, small portions are usually sufficient, particularly when served with a rich, sweet dessert.

Although some people endorse it, I find the pairing of chocolate with red wine to be misguided. The chocolate tends to rob the wine of its fruit, while accentuating its astringent qualities of alcohol and tannin. If you must drink red wine with chocolate, try port, a sweet fortified wine.

wine-baked stuffed apples

SUGGESTED WINE: MOSCATO OR PORT | MAKES 6 SERVINGS

Trees laden with apples are harbingers of autumn in wine country. Choose Baldwin, Cortland, Golden Delicious, or other good baking apples.

INGREDIENTS

6 large, firm baking apples (see recipe introduction)

$1/2$ cup crushed Amaretti (page 134) or other crisp cookies

$1/3$ cup dried cranberries or currants

3 tablespoons brown sugar

3 tablespoons unsalted butter, melted

1 tablespoon freshly squeezed lemon juice

$1^1/2$ teaspoons ground cinnamon

1 cup Chenin Blanc or Moscato

Heavy (whipping) cream, light cream, or half-and-half for serving

Preheat an oven to 350 degrees F.

Select a baking dish just large enough to hold all of the apples without touching.

Trim the bottoms of the apples if necessary to stand the fruits upright. Remove about ½ inch of the peel around the top of each apple, then core the apples, being careful not to go all the way through to the bottoms.

In a bowl, combine the cookies, cranberries or currants, sugar, butter, lemon juice, and cinnamon and mix well. Spoon the filling, dividing equally, into the cored apples. Transfer the apples to the reserved baking dish.

Pour the wine over the apples, cover the pan with a tight-fitting lid or aluminum foil, and bake for 30 minutes. Uncover and continue to bake, basting occasionally with the pan juices, until the apples are tender when pierced with a wooden skewer but still hold their shape, about 30 minutes longer.

Serve warm or at room temperature. Pass a pitcher of cream to pour over the apples at the table.

goat's milk flan

SUGGESTED WINE: MOSCATO OR LATE-HARVEST RIESLING | MAKES **8** SERVINGS

Tangy goat's milk adds a new dimension to this popular dessert introduced to the valley by early settlers from Mexico. The French call their similar classic crème caramel, *and the Italians know it as* crema caramella.

If desired, the caramel syrup and the custard mixture can be evenly divided among eight 6-ounce custard cups. It can also be served warm, about 20 minutes after it comes out of the oven.

INGREDIENTS

1^3/$_4$ cups sugar

5 egg yolks

3 whole eggs

3 cups fresh goat's milk, or 2 cans (12^1/$_2$ ounces each) evaporated goat's milk

2 teaspoons pure vanilla extract

Position racks so that the custard will bake in the middle of an oven and preheat the oven to 350 degrees F. Select a 9-by-2-inch round cake pan and set aside. Position a large bowl of iced water alongside the stove top.

In a heavy saucepan, preferably made of stainless steel or copper, combine 1 cup of the sugar and ¼ cup water and stir well. Place over medium heat, cover, and heat for about 4 minutes. Remove the cover and continue to cook without disturbing the mixture until it begins to color, then continue cooking, slowly swirling the pan occasionally to spread the color evenly, until the syrup turns a rich amber; this will take about 8 minutes after removing the cover from the pan. If sugar crystals begin to form around the sides of the pan just above the bubbling syrup, brush them away with a pastry brush moistened with water. As soon as the syrup reaches the desired color, briefly place the pan in the iced water to halt the cooking.

Carefully pour the hot caramel syrup into the reserved cake pan and immediately swirl to coat the bottom and about one-third of the way up the sides. Set the pan aside to cool; the syrup will harden very quickly.

In a large bowl, combine the egg yolks and eggs and beat lightly with a fork just until well blended. Avoid overbeating at any point to prevent too many air bubbles from forming. Slowly stir in the goat's milk, then the remaining ¾ cup sugar and the vanilla. Slowly pour the mixture through a fine-mesh strainer into the syrup-lined pan.

Place the pan on a rack set in a large, deep baking pan, transfer to the oven, and pour enough hot (not boiling) water into the large pan to reach about halfway up the sides of the custard container. Place a sheet of aluminum foil over the pan to cover the top of the custard loosely.

Bake until the custard is set but still wobbles like gelatin when the pan is shaken very gently, 1 to 1½ hours. Regulate the oven temperature during baking to maintain water at the almost-simmering stage; do not allow to boil.

Transfer the custard pan from the water bath to a wire rack to cool to room temperature, then cover tightly and refrigerate until well chilled, at least 3 hours or for up to overnight.

Just before serving, dip the bottom of the pan in a bowl of hot water for about 30 seconds. Run a thin, flexible knife blade or metal spatula around the inside edge of the pan. Invert a serving plate over the pan, invert the plate and pan together, and carefully lift off the pan. The caramel syrup will run down the sides and onto the serving plate to surround the custard.

To serve, cut into wedges and spoon some of the syrup over each portion.

lavender gelato

SUGGESTED WINE: MOSCATO OR SPARKLING WINE | MAKES ABOUT **1** QUART FOR **6** TO **8** SERVINGS

On a warm summer day, the heady fragrance of profusely blooming lavender perfumes many Napa Valley gardens. I enjoy capturing the essence of that delightful fragrance in this rich ice cream. And please see the vanilla variation that follows the recipe for my favorite flavoring.

Double the mixture if you have a 2-quart ice cream maker.

INGREDIENTS

2 cups whole milk

2 cups heavy (whipping) cream

6 tablespoons finely chopped fresh pesticide-free lavender flowers, or 3 tablespoons crumbled dried lavender flowers

Zest of 1 lemon, removed in long strips

7 egg yolks

1 cup sugar

$1/4$ teaspoon salt

Purple food coloring paste (optional)

In a heavy saucepan, combine the milk, cream, lavender, and lemon zest. Place over medium heat and bring the mixture almost to the boiling point, then remove from the heat and set aside to steep and cool to room temperature, 30 to 45 minutes.

Pour the milk-cream mixture through a fine-mesh strainer into a clean saucepan and discard the strained solids. Place over medium heat and return almost to the boiling point.

Meanwhile, in the bottom pan of a double boiler (or a pan that a metal bowl can nest inside to create a double-boiler arrangement), pour in water to a depth of about 1 inch. Place over high heat and bring to a simmer, then adjust the heat to keep the water simmering barely. Place a metal bowl in a larger bowl of iced water and set aside.

recipe continues >>

>>

In the top pan of the double boiler (or a metal bowl that can nest inside the pan of simmering water), combine the egg yolks, sugar, and salt. Beat with a hand mixer at medium-high speed until the mixture is pale yellow and creamy, about 3 minutes. Pour the hot milk-cream mixture through a fine-mesh strainer into a heatproof pitcher. With the mixer running, slowly add the hot milk-cream mixture to the egg mixture and beat until smooth. Place the pan (or nest the bowl) over the simmering water and stir the mixture constantly until it is thick enough to coat the back of a spoon (your finger should leave a trail when you run it across the spoon), about 15 minutes; do not allow to boil.

Pour through a fine-mesh strainer into the bowl set in iced water. Place a piece of plastic wrap directly onto the surface of the custard to prevent a skin from forming and set aside to cool for about 15 minutes. Remove the bowl from the iced water and discard the plastic wrap. If desired, stir in just a touch of food coloring paste to create a pale lavender hue. Cover tightly, and refrigerate until well chilled, at least 3 hours or, preferably, overnight.

Pour the chilled custard mixture into an ice cream maker and freeze according to the manufacturer's instructions. Serve when the ice cream holds together but is still soft. Or, for a firmer texture, pack the ice cream into a container with a tight-fitting lid and place in a freezer for several hours or for up to several days. Transfer the freezer container to a refrigerator for a few minutes before you plan to serve the ice cream to allow it to reach the proper consistency. (Alternatively, microwave the ice cream for about 20 seconds at high power to soften if frozen hard.) If the ice cream gets icy from long freezer storage, whip it with a whisk just before serving.

VANILLA VARIATION

Omit the lavender, lemon zest, and food coloring. Split 1 vanilla bean lengthwise and scrape the seeds into the milk-cream mixture. Toss in the bean as well and heat and steep as directed. Stir 1 teaspoon pure vanilla extract into the cooled custard before chilling.

triple cream tiramisu

SUGGESTED WINE: SUTTER HOME TRIPLE CREAM | MAKES 8 SERVINGS

Sutter Home Triple Cream dessert wine (see page 132) mellows well with espresso and mascarpone, the velvety Italian triple-cream cheese, to create this spirited version of the ever-popular Italian "pick-me-up." If Triple Cream is not available, substitute brandy, a favorite liqueur, or strongly brewed coffee.

Traditionally, the dessert is made with dry, crisp Italian ladyfingers that quickly soak up the dipping liquid. Feel free to substitute softer homemade or bakery versions, or use pieces of sponge cake or other plain cake. The amount of dipping liquid needed will vary with the type of cookies or cake used.

INGREDIENTS

1 1/4 cups Sutter Home Triple Cream

1/4 cup instant espresso, preferably Medaglia d'Oro brand

1 1/2 pounds mascarpone cheese

1 cup heavy (whipping) cream

1/2 cup sugar

Pinch of salt

About 30 ladyfingers

4 ounces finest-quality semisweet chocolate,
	finely grated or shaved

In a small saucepan, place 1 cup of the Triple Cream over medium heat and bring to a simmer. Add the instant espresso and stir until dissolved. Pour into a shallow bowl and set aside to cool completely.

In a bowl, combine the remaining 1/4 cup Triple Cream, the mascarpone, cream, sugar, and salt. Whisk or beat with a hand mixer at medium speed until the mixture is the consistency of softly whipped cream. Do not overbeat. Set aside.

Working with 1 ladyfinger at a time, dip the cookies into the cold Triple Cream–espresso mixture and completely line the bottom of an 8-inch baking pan or dish with them. Use broken ladyfingers to fill any large holes. Spoon in about half of the mascarpone mixture and sprinkle with about half of the chocolate. Dip the remaining ladyfingers and arrange them in a single layer atop the mascarpone. Top with the remaining mascarpone mixture and sprinkle evenly with the remaining chocolate. Cover tightly with plastic wrap and refrigerate for at least 3 hours or for up to overnight.

To serve, spoon into individual dishes.

chilled triple cream zabaglione

SUGGESTED WINE: SUTTER HOME TRIPLE CREAM | MAKES **6** SERVINGS

This Trinchero family version of the traditional Italian whipped wine custard is cooled and stabilized with whipped cream. Unlike the last-minute preparation necessary for the better-known frothy warm zabaglione, this one can be made the night before serving. Set out a plate of Amaretti (page 134) or other crisp cookies.

Triple Cream, a sherry-based dessert wine infused with herbs and spices and made from a century-old secret family recipe, is sold only at the winery tasting room. You may substitute Marsala to make traditional zabaglione.

INGREDIENTS

6 egg yolks

6 tablespoons sugar

1/2 cup Sutter Home Triple Cream

1 cup heavy (whipping) cream

6 maraschino cherries for garnish (optional)

Place a metal bowl in a freezer to chill.

In the bottom pan of a double boiler (or a pan that a metal bowl can nest inside to create a double-boiler arrangement), pour in water to a depth of about 1 inch. Place over high heat and bring to a simmer, then adjust the heat to keep the water simmering barely.

In the top pan of the double boiler (or a metal bowl that can nest inside the pan of simmering water), beat the egg yolks with a hand mixer at medium-high speed or a whisk until blended. While continuing to beat or whisk, add the sugar, 1 tablespoon at a time, then gradually beat or whisk in the wine.

Place the pan (or nest the bowl) over the simmering water and beat or whisk the custard until thickened, 3 to 4 minutes. Remove from the simmering water and set aside to cool completely. Wash and dry the beaters or whisk and place in the freezer to chill.

In the chilled bowl with the chilled beaters or whisk, whip the cream just until firm peaks form when the beater is raised; be very careful not to overbeat. Fold the whipped cream into the cooled custard, incorporating well. Spoon the mixture into individual dessert bowls or wine goblets. (At this point the servings can be covered tightly with plastic wrap and refrigerated for up to 24 hours.)

Just before serving, garnish each serving with a cherry (if using).

amaretti

SUGGESTED WINE: SUTTER HOME TRIPLE CREAM OR PORT | MAKES ABOUT **3** DOZEN AMARETTI

Bob Trinchero still waxes nostalgically about his childhood recollections of these crisp almond cookies baked by his Uncle Ernest, then a chef in Manhattan. The Trincheros serve these popular Italian-style macaroons with the family's Triple Cream dessert wine (see page 132).

INGREDIENTS

1 cup blanched almonds

1$\frac{1}{2}$ cups sugar

$\frac{1}{4}$ cup egg whites (from about 2 eggs)

$\frac{1}{4}$ teaspoon salt

1 teaspoon pure almond extract

Whole blanched almonds or pine nuts for decorating (optional)

Position racks so that the cookies will bake in the middle of an oven and preheat the oven to 350 degrees F. Line 2 or more baking sheets with kitchen parchment and set aside.

In a food processor, combine the almonds and $\frac{1}{2}$ cup of the sugar and grind to a fine powder. Set aside.

In a bowl, beat the egg whites with a hand mixer at medium-high speed until very foamy. Add the ground almonds, the remaining 1 cup sugar, the salt, and almond extract and beat with the mixer at medium speed until the mixture is fairly smooth and holds together, about 2 minutes.

Using a 1-tablespoon ice cream scoop, place mounds of the dough about 2 inches apart on the prepared baking sheets. Using your fingertips, lightly flatten each dough mound to form a round about 1½ inches in diameter. Top each round with a whole almond or a few pine nuts (if using).

Bake until the cookies are lightly browned, about 20 minutes.

Transfer the baking sheets to a wire rack to cool for 8 to 10 minutes. Using your hands, carefully peel the paper off the backs of the cookies and transfer to the rack to cool completely.

spiced persimmon-walnut cookies

SUGGESTED WINE: SUTTER HOME TRIPLE CREAM OR PORT | MAKES ABOUT 5 DOZEN COOKIES

One of my indelible images of autumn in Napa Valley is of leafless persimmon trees laden with shiny orange fruits against clear, brilliant blue skies. In this Trinchero family recipe, the persimmon pulp adds moistness, beautiful color, and a delicate flavor to the cakelike cookies. Although I prefer butter over vegetable shortening, Evalyn Trinchero uses the latter for the lightly sweetened cookies.

INGREDIENTS

2 cups all-purpose flour

1 teaspoon baking soda

1/2 teaspoon salt

1 teaspoon ground cinnamon

1/2 teaspoon freshly grated nutmeg

1/2 cup (1 stick) unsalted butter or solid vegetable shortening,
    at room temperature

1 cup sugar

1 egg

1 cup persimmon puree, from 2 to 3 very ripe
    Hachiya persimmons

1 teaspoon pure vanilla extract

1 cup walnuts, finely chopped

1 cup raisins

Position racks so that the cookies will bake in the middle of an oven and preheat the oven to 350 degrees F. Line 2 or more baking sheets with kitchen parchment and set aside.

Place the flour, baking soda, salt, cinnamon, and nutmeg together in a strainer or sifter and sift into a large bowl.

Whisk to blend well and set aside.

In a bowl, combine the butter or shortening and sugar and beat with an electric mixer at medium-high speed until light and fluffy. Add the egg, persimmon puree, and vanilla and beat until creamy smooth.

Using the mixer on low speed, add the flour mixture to the persimmon mixture and blend until smooth. Stir in the nuts and raisins.

Drop the batter by rounded teaspoonfuls, placing them about 1 inch apart, onto the prepared baking sheets. Bake the cookies until puffed and browned, about 20 minutes.

Transfer the baking sheets to a wire rack to cool for about 5 minutes. Using a spatula, transfer the cookies to the rack to cool completely.

lemon roulade with strawberries and whipped cream

SUGGESTED WINE: MOSCATO OR SPARKLING WINE | MAKES 8 SERVINGS

This springtime dessert, often prepared by pastry chef Susanne Salvestrin for Sutter Home special events, makes a beautiful presentation that belies its ease of preparation. The lemon curd can be made ahead and the sponge cake bakes in only 10 minutes.

INGREDIENTS

LEMON CURD

1 cup granulated sugar

8 egg yolks

$1/2$ cup freshly squeezed lemon juice, strained of pulp

2 teaspoons finely grated or minced fresh lemon zest

$1/2$ cup (1 stick) unsalted butter, at room temperature,
    cut into small pieces

SPONGE CAKE

Cooking spray for greasing

Powdered sugar for dusting

1 cup sifted cake flour

1 teaspoon baking powder

$1/4$ teaspoon salt

3 egg yolks

1 cup granulated sugar

2 teaspoons pure vanilla extract

5 egg whites

Powdered sugar for dusting

Whipped cream

2 cups chopped strawberries

8 whole strawberries, thinly sliced almost through to
    the stem end and fanned out, for garnish

8 fresh mint sprigs for garnish

To make the Lemon Curd, in the bottom pan of a double boiler (or a pan that a metal bowl can nest inside to create a double-boiler arrangement), pour in water to a depth of about 1 inch. Place over high heat and bring to a simmer, then adjust the heat to keep the water simmering barely.

recipe continues

In the top pan of the double boiler (or a metal bowl that can nest inside the pan of simmering water), combine the sugar and egg yolks and stir to blend well. Stir in the lemon juice and zest. Place the pan (or nest the bowl) over the simmering water, add the butter, and cook, stirring constantly, until the mixture is thick enough to coat the back of a spoon (your finger should leave a trail when you run it across the spoon) but remains pourable, 10 to 15 minutes. To prevent the eggs from curdling, do not allow the mixture to approach a boil.

Pour the curd into a bowl. Immediately place a piece of plastic wrap directly onto the surface of the curd to prevent a skin from forming. Set aside to cool completely, then discard the plastic wrap, cover tightly, and refrigerate for up to 3 weeks.

To make the Sponge Cake, position racks so that the cake will bake in the middle of an oven and preheat the oven to 400 degrees F. Coat a 15-by-10-by-1-inch jelly-roll pan lightly with cooking spray and line it with kitchen parchment or waxed paper, then spray the paper and set aside. Lightly dust a cloth kitchen towel with powdered sugar and set aside.

Place the flour, baking powder, and salt together in a strainer or sifter and sift into a bowl. Whisk to mix well and set aside.

In the bowl of a stand mixer fitted with a flat beater, or in a bowl with a hand mixer, beat the egg yolks at high speed for about 1 minute. Gradually add ¾ cup of the granulated sugar and continue beating at high speed until the mixture is thick and creamy and forms a wide ribbon when some of the mixture is lifted and dropped back over the remainder, about 5 minutes if using a stand mixer, or about 10 minutes if using a hand mixer. Add ¼ cup water and the vanilla and blend well. Set aside.

Using the stand mixer fitted with a wire whip or a hand mixer with clean beaters, in a clean metal bowl, beat the egg whites at low speed until frothy bubbles cover the surface. Increase the speed to medium and beat until very soft, billowy mounds form when the beater is slowly raised. With the mixer running, gradually add the remaining ¼ cup sugar, about 1 tablespoon at a time, and beat until the whites form peaks that are stiff but still moist when the beater is raised.

Immediately sift the flour mixture over the egg yolk mixture. Then add one-fourth of the egg whites and, using a large balloon whisk or rubber spatula, quickly and gently fold in the mixture just until the flour mixture and whites disappear. In the same way, gently fold in the remaining whites; avoid overblending, which will deflate the batter.

Scrape the batter into the prepared pan and smooth the surface with a rubber spatula. Bake until the cake springs back when lightly touched in the center with your fingertip and a wooden skewer inserted in several places throughout the cake comes out clean, about 10 minutes.

Remove the pan to a work surface. Run a metal spatula or table knife around the inside edge to loosen the cake from the pan. Invert the cake onto the sugar-dusted towel and peel off the paper. Starting from the narrow end, roll the cake up in the towel. Place seam side down and set aside to cool completely.

Carefully unroll the cooled cake on a work surface, remove the towel, and spread the cake with the lemon curd. Re-roll the cake as compactly as possible. Slide a large cake spatula or rimless baking sheet underneath the cake and transfer it, seam side down, to a serving platter. Cover and refrigerate for up to several hours.

To serve, dust individual plates with powdered sugar. Slice the cake into 8 equal pieces and place a piece in the center of each plate. Spoon a dollop of whipped cream a little off-center onto each piece of cake and sprinkle ¼ cup chopped strawberries over each serving of cake and cream. Garnish each plate with a fanned strawberry and mint sprig.

upside-down peach babycakes

SUGGESTED WINE: MOSCATO OR LATE-HARVEST RIESLING | MAKES **6** SERVINGS

Susanne Salvestrin often bakes these quick-and-easy individual cakes to serve with breakfast at the Sutter Home Inn. They're equally delicious made with apples, blueberries, or other fruits and served as a treat at any time of day.

Nonstick miniature Bundt cake pans, with 6 wells per pan, are readily available in cookware stores. A muffin pan with oversized cups can be used instead.

INGREDIENTS

Cooking spray for greasing

6 tablespoons brown sugar

About 4 small ripe peaches, peeled, pitted, and chopped

$1^3/_4$ cups all-purpose flour

1 teaspoon baking powder

$^1/_2$ teaspoon baking soda

$^1/_4$ teaspoon salt

$^3/_4$ cup buttermilk

$^3/_4$ cup mild honey or pure maple syrup

$^1/_4$ cup canola or other high-quality vegetable oil

2 tablespoons pure vanilla extract

1 tablespoon freshly squeezed lemon juice

Position racks so that the cakes will bake in the middle of an oven and preheat the oven to 350 degrees F. Coat six 1-cup nonstick miniature Bundt-pan or muffin-pan wells (see recipe introduction) with cooking spray.

Sprinkle 1 tablespoon of the brown sugar onto the bottom of each well and spoon in just enough peaches to cover the bottoms. Set aside.

In a bowl, combine the flour, baking powder, baking soda, and salt and whisk to blend well.

In a separate bowl, combine the buttermilk, honey or syrup, oil, vanilla, and lemon juice and blend well. Pour the buttermilk mixture into the flour mixture and stir just until blended. Spoon the batter over the peaches in each well, dividing equally.

Bake until a wooden skewer inserted into the thickest part of each cake comes out clean, 25 to 30 minutes.

Remove the pan to a work surface and let stand for about 2 minutes. Run a metal spatula or table knife around the inside edge of each well to loosen the cakes. Invert a wire rack over the pan, invert the pan and rack together, and carefully remove the pan. Set the cakes aside to cool for a few minutes.

Serve the cakes warm or at room temperature.

country pear pie

SUGGESTED WINE: MOSCATO OR LATE-HARVEST RIESLING | MAKES **6** SERVINGS

Evalyn Trinchero makes this unique pie when Bartlett pears are at their peak at the St. Helena farmers' market. During baking, a simple mixture of kitchen staples is transformed into a dense pudding- like filling that surrounds the tender fruit. Serve with vanilla gelato (page 130), frozen yogurt, or whipped cream.

During pear season, consider freezing a few extra pies for later enjoyment. After baking, cool thoroughly and wrap well in plastic freezer wrap; thaw at room temperature for at least 4 hours prior to serving, then preheat an oven to 200 degrees F and warm the pie for 10 to 15 minutes.

INGREDIENTS

9-inch unbaked pie crust (use a favorite recipe or commercial crust)

3 ripe but firm pears, peeled, cored, and halved

2 eggs

1 cup sugar

$^1/_2$ cup all-purpose flour

Pinch of salt

$^1/_4$ cup ($^1/_2$ stick) unsalted butter, melted and cooled slightly

1 teaspoon pure vanilla extract

Prepare the pie crust and set aside.

Position racks so that the pie will bake in the middle of an oven and preheat the oven to 350 degrees F.

Place the pear halves in a spoke pattern in the pie crust, flat side down.

In a bowl, lightly beat the eggs. Add the sugar, flour, salt, butter, and vanilla and beat until smooth. Pour the mixture over the pears in the pie crust.

Bake until the filling is set, 1 hour to 1½ hours, depending upon the juiciness of the pears. To test for doneness, using a small, sharp knife, break through the crisp top layer that forms during baking to create a small hole in the center of the pie, then insert the knife into the filling; it should come out slightly gooey, but not wet. If the crust begins to over-brown during baking, cover the rim with a ring of aluminum foil or a pie crust shield.

Transfer the pie to a wire rack to cool. Serve warm or at room temperature.

autumn apple or pear crisp

SUGGESTED WINE: MOSCATO OR PORT | MAKES 8 SERVINGS

Each autumn the apple and pear orchard at Villa Sunshine bore so much fruit that my partner, Andrew, and I gave away basketfuls to our family and friends. Here is one of our favorite uses of the fruit we kept, a recipe adapted by Andrew from one published in a column by friend and fellow cookbook author Marion Cunningham. We agree with Marion that the crispy topping is the only one worthy of the name.

Choose flavorful baking apples such as Baldwin, Cortland, Golden Delicious, Gravenstein, Ida Red, or local heirloom varieties. Select pears such as Bartlett, Bosc, or Comice that are ripe but firm. Whether you choose apples or pears, always serve the crisp with lightly sweetened softly whipped cream, Lavender Gelato (page 129), or vanilla gelato (page 130).

INGREDIENTS

6 cups peeled, cored, and sliced apples or pears (see recipe introduction)

1 cup high-quality raisins, preferably from a farmers' market

$1/2$ to $3/4$ cup light brown sugar, depending upon sweetness of apples or pears

1 to 2 tablespoons freshly squeezed lemon juice, depending upon sweetness of apples or pears

2 tablespoons cornstarch, potato starch, or quick-cooking tapioca

1 tablespoon ground cinnamon (optional)

CRISP TOPPING

1 cup all-purpose flour

1 cup granulated sugar

$1/2$ teaspoon salt

1 egg, lightly beaten

$1/2$ cup (1 stick) unsalted butter, melted

Position racks so that the crisp will bake in the middle of an oven and preheat the oven to 375 degrees F. Select a 13-by-9-inch baking dish and set aside.

In a bowl, combine the apples or pears, raisins, brown sugar, and lemon juice and toss well. Sprinkle with the cornstarch, potato starch, or tapioca and the cinnamon (if using) and mix well. Set aside.

To make the Crisp Topping, in a bowl, combine the flour, sugar, and salt and mix well. Using a pastry blender or fork, cut in the egg until thoroughly combined and the mixture resembles fine bread crumbs.

Stir the apple or pear mixture well, transfer to the reserved baking dish, and spread in an even layer. Distribute the flour mixture evenly over the fruit, then drizzle the melted butter evenly over the topping.

Bake until the topping is golden brown and crisp, 35 to 45 minutes.

Remove the pan to a wire rack to cool for about 10 minutes. Serve warm.

acknowledgments

To **STAN HOCK**, director of communications at Sutter Home Winery and a consummate gentleman, for putting this project together and overseeing it with great skill and efficiency, and for his research for the text.

To the **TRINCHERO FAMILY**, especially **EVALYN** and **BOB, MARY**, and **GINA MEE**, for gathering and contributing their favorite recipes and for their generosity to the life and culture of Napa Valley.

To the chefs at Sutter Home, **JEFFREY STARR** and **SUSANNE SALVESTRIN**, for sharing their innovative creations.

To the staff of **CHRONICLE BOOKS** for their good work in producing this book, especially **STEPHANIE ROSENBAUM** for keeping everything running smoothly.

To copyeditor **SHARON SILVA**, for once again refining my words.

To my Napa Valley family, **MARTHA MᶜNAIR, JOHN RICHARDSON, DEVERUX MᶜNAIR**, and **RYAN RICHARDSON**, for their hospitality during my visits to St. Helena.

To the book designer, **STEFANIE HERMSDORF**, and photographers, **ZEVA OELBAUM** and **M. J. WICKHAM**, for creating a stunning setting for the text and recipes.

To my partner, **ANDREW MOORE**, for his very able work on the manuscript and recipe testing.

table of equivalents

The exact equivalents in the following tables have been rounded for convenience.

LIQUID | DRY MEASURES

U.S.	METRIC
$1/4$ teaspoon	1.25 milliliters
$1/2$ teaspoon	2.5 milliliters
1 teaspoon	5 milliliters
1 tablespoon (3 teaspoons)	15 milliliters
1 fluid ounce (2 tablespoons)	30 milliliters
$1/4$ cup	60 milliliters
$1/3$ cup	80 milliliters
$1/2$ cup	120 milliliters
1 cup	240 milliliters
1 pint (2 cups)	480 milliliters
1 quart (4 cups, 32 ounces)	960 milliliters
1 gallon (4 quarts)	3.84 liters
1 ounce (by weight)	28 grams
1 pound	454 grams
2.2 pounds	1 kilogram

LENGTH

U.S.	METRIC
$1/8$ inch	3 millimeters
$1/4$ inch	6 millimeters
$1/2$ inch	12 millimeters
1 inch	2.5 centimeters

OVEN TEMPERATURE

FAHRENHEIT	CELSIUS	GAS
250	120	$1/2$
275	140	1
300	150	2
325	160	3
350	180	4
375	190	5
400	200	6
425	220	7
450	230	8
475	240	9
500	260	10